45

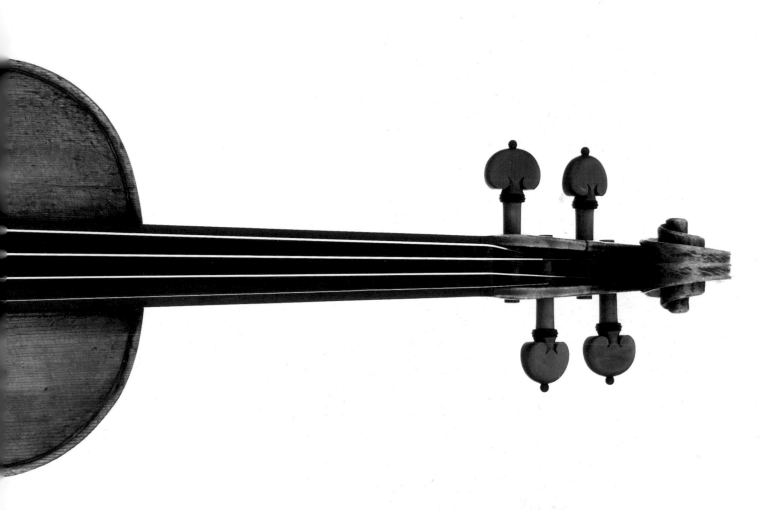

Haynes

Violin
Manual

Haynes Publishing

© John Gosling & Marcus Corrie 2014

John Gosling & Marcus Corrie have asserted their right to be identified as the authors of this work

First published in July 2014

A catalogue record for this book is available from the British Library

ISBN 978 0 85733 379 7

Library of Congress catalog card no. 2014930858

Published by Haynes Publishing,
Sparkford, Yeovil, Somerset BA22 7JJ, UK

Tel: 01963 442030 Fax: 01963 440001
Int. tel: +44 1963 442030 Int. fax: +44 1963 440001
E-mail: sales@haynes.co.uk
Website: www.haynes.co.uk

Haynes North America, Inc.,
861 Lawrence Drive, Newbury Park,
California 91320, USA

Printed in the USA by Odcombe Press LP,
1299 Bridgestone Parkway, La Vergne, TN 37086

Haynes

Violin
Manual

**How to assess, buy,
set-up and maintain
your violin**

John Gosling
Marcus Corrie

Contents

RIGHT del Gesu Ole Bull 1744

About the authors

John Gosling

Coming from a long lineage of fine woodworking, John studied violin making, restoration and repair at Newark School of Violin Making. After graduating he studied under his brother Paul Gosling and then opened Chapel Violins workshop in Newark, dedicated to fine instrument supply, restoration and repair. The school was opened shortly after, offering a variety of repair and restoration courses, training students to a professional level. John also tutored at Newark School before deciding to work full-time teaching and restoring at Chapel Violins.

John is an active board member of the British Violin Making Association (BVMA) and has contributed several articles to *Strad* magazine on restoring and making violins. John is also an avid antique and art collector and is a regular at local antique shows.

Marcus Corrie

Marcus studied astrophysics at Leicester University before entering the IT industry, specialising in 3D graphics and technical authoring. He then spent a further 10 years working in the gaming industry, meanwhile studying violin making and violins at an amateur level. Marcus took a full-time course at the Newark School to study to a professional level and joined Chapel Violins, where he continues his education under John at the workshop.

Marcus takes an interest in many other diverse subjects ranging from dendrochronology (tree-ring dating) to the manufacture and restoration of other musical instruments, including percussion and guitars. He is married with a long-suffering wife and young son.

Introduction

Karolina Radziej (*Trio Nightingale*)

The violin is one of the most expressive and controllable instruments ever invented and it is found in the widest imaginable range of music genres. It is not difficult to make a violin produce a sound (as close neighbours may agree), but it requires years of practice to use a violin to express music and emotion properly.

The violin has been with us in its present form since the 16th century, and over the 400 years of its existence it has been very widely played and enjoyed, from the elegant courts of kings to the tawdriest tavern. It has touched the hearts of players, collectors and makers alike.

With values ranging from that of a good-quality lump of firewood to the pinnacle of violin making worth millions, the violin has also caressed and emptied the wallets of the wealthy.

In May 2006, a Stradivari violin sold for over £1.8 million – quite a lot to spend on an instrument!

Worshipped by collectors, nurtured by players, studied by makers, and for want of a better term, dealt with by dealers, the violin is an instrument of great appeal.

However, you do not need to be able to play the violin like a virtuoso in order to work on the violin as a piece of fine woodwork, and likewise you do not need to be able to service a violin in order to play it. As a player, though, there are certain things you can do to keep your violin in great condition, and as a maker/repairer/restorer, at any level, it really helps if you can play a few notes.

This book will not help you learn to play, but it will infuse you with a wealth of knowledge and experience in how to select, care for and maintain a violin.

CHAPTER 1

The violin and its makers

The origins of the modern violin can be traced back through the centuries beyond the cultures of Renaissance Europe into the times of the Byzantine and Moor empires. In essence the modern violin is the culmination of human experimentation and knowledge passed on from craftsman to craftsman, emerging from the collaboration of minds separated by time, country and language, but unified by the desire to create a really good sound with a beautiful-looking instrument. The design of the modern violin was driven by the evolution of music and performance in Europe, with playing style, tone and loudness all having played a part.

Origins

The violin finds its origins in Moorish instruments from the northern African and Arabian tribes. The rebab and rebec were popular folk instruments with a simple sound box and only a couple of strings, played with a primitive bow for the entertainment of small audiences, combined with singing and drumming.

The Moors is a collective name for tribes from the Islamic empire and they spread from northern Africa into Aragon, establishing influence across the Mediterranean. For 700 years they flourished in what is now modern Spain, bringing with them their instrument technology from which many Western instruments are derived; for example, the lute comes from the Arabic al'oud, which is a similar bowl-shaped, stringed instrument.

BELOW Patio of Arraynes of Alhambra, Granada, Spain. *Toniflapl*

There are many artistic depictions of rebabs in paintings and drawings of that era originating from instruments made in Aragon. Rebab means 'bowed instrument' in Arabic and was probably used to describe a range of different designs. Fundamentally the rebab was played in a vertical position with a bow, while the rebec, another instrument of Arabian/Moorish origin, was played on the shoulder. The rebab had a very limited tonal range, with only one octave possible, which meant that it became obsolete as music evolved.

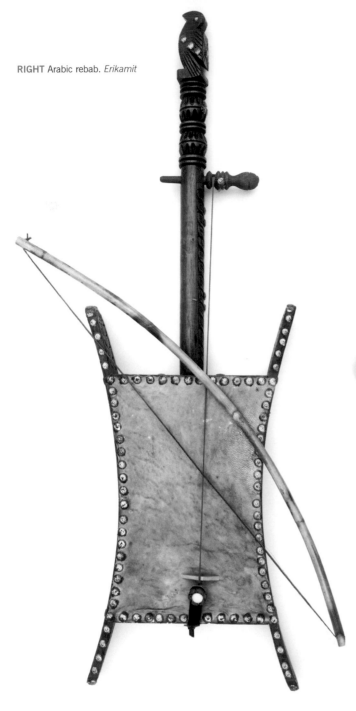

The Moors were gradually driven out of the Spanish peninsula and by the middle of the 15th century their culture had been subsumed, but they left behind their traditions of instrument making and playing that influenced the design of the violin in the 17th and 18th centuries.

The Byzantine Empire, which dominated the eastern Mediterranean until the middle of the 15th century, had a similar instrument called the lyra da braccio. This instrument was played on the arms in much the same way as the rebec or up on the shoulder as depicted in drawings and paintings of the time.

Both the lyra da braccio and rebec designs flowed into the creative melting pot of the Mediterranean from the expansion and subjugation of the Byzantine and Moor civilisations. These cultures were instrumental in the sudden creative explosion that occurred at the beginning of the Renaissance, and they were essential ingredients in the literature, philosophy and art of that time that ultimately influenced the design of the modern violin.

During the Renaissance period, it is thought that instrument ideas combined to converge on the more modern form of the violin we have today, and the viol and lute makers of the day turned their attention to creating this new design of instrument. Already skilled in creating viola d'amore (perhaps a corruption of 'viola of the Moors') and viol da gamba ('viol of the leg'), these instrument makers, through natural progression, created the shape of violin, viola and cello with which we are familiar today. Individual components of the violin each underwent their own evolution towards optimal design.

Evidence suggests that the innovative Andrea Amati developed the first true violin form in the early 16th century. This underwent further refinement through the Amati, Guarneri and Stradivari families, and spread still further among other brilliant yet less-well-known craftsmen, each interpreting form and design in their own way – but none, it seems, surpassed the supreme quality of Stradivari.

Fuelled by the popularity of the instrument, first with royal courts, then with the gentry and populace, violin manufacture flourished. Violin-making establishments became prevalent throughout Europe on an industrial scale. Skip forwards in time to today and we find that the violin is still an extremely popular instrument, the design of which is relatively unchanged by time.

Schools and styles

Regions of violin manufacture can be loosely described as having 'styles', which are termed 'schools' in the trade. These can be recognised by certain identification fingerprints, which are not without exception and therefore should be used as a rule of thumb.

In this section we give examples of some of the most famous and well-documented makers, but it must be emphasised that there are hundreds of makers from these schools, and therefore readers interested to know more than this humble introduction can provide are urged to do their own research into the different styles and schools.

It is also necessary to put schools into the context of their period, when bubonic plague ravaged Europe and took thousands to early graves. Families of craftsmen were decimated by the horrors of the plague, and the only way to continue business and tradition was to take on apprentices from other families that showed promise. This is probably how knowledge and trade secrets were propagated and how new businesses arose in the regions that we will now discuss.

Italian schools

Viol making in Italy was well established around the 15th century. Italian violin making was heavily influenced by the Renaissance period, which brought renewed interest in the arts and new forms of music played in palaces and churches, leading to growing demand for instruments of good quality. Around this time the great composers were creating their masterpieces for the court, and violin makers of the period sought patronage by wealthy aristocrats and the Church.

There is much in common between the Italian violin makers, largely due to the apprenticeship model of education and employment whereby would-be craftsmen would learn their trade from an established maker, and then subtly evolve the design to make their own mark, with f-holes, scrollwork and purfling each showing characteristics of individual makers.

The Italians are particularly noted for their varnish and finish. Most, if not all, instruments from Cremona in this period

RIGHT Gasparo da Salo 1560c

Courtesy of the Chi Mei Museum, Taiwan

were finished with a most magnificent varnish, the secret of its ingredients all but lost to time. The early instruments were amber in colour and later violins were a light red, while Neapolitan varnish was yellow. Whether varnish has any effect on tonal quality we leave for the reader's ear to judge, but we can all agree on the aesthetic appeal of classic Italian varnish.

Brescian schools
Gasparo da Salo (1542–1609) was one of the earliest violin makers. Born Gasparo Bertolotti, he was originally a viol maker and was considered to be the founder of the Brescian school of violin making. He is credited with being one of the earliest instrument makers to take pride in workmanship and elevate the craft to a true art form. His varnish was generally a light brown colour with a red tint.

Giovanni Paolo Maggini (c1580–c1630), who studied under Gasparo da Salo, evolved his own particular way of doing things beyond the original da Salo designs – which seems to have been very much the trend in pupils of makers. Maggini ornamented many of his instruments and in some cases inlaid a double row of purfling. He succumbed to the bubonic plague after creating some 60 violins.

Neapolitan schools
Alessandro Gagliano (1640–1725) studied under Antonio Stradivari in Cremona and was founder of the Gagliano family of violin makers in his home town of Naples. Paolo Grancino (1665–1692), who possibly studied under Nicolo Amati, was father of the Grancino family of violin makers.

Cremonese schools
The Cremonese school is perhaps the most famous of the Italian schools, if only for one man's fame. Antonio Stradivari (1644–1737) was the leading figure in improving the quality and sound of the violin. It is speculated that Stradivari was

BELOW Cremona today. *Karol Kozlowski*

BELOW Stradivari 1709 Viotti Marie

RIGHT Guarneri,
Giuseppe del Gesu
1733.

Courtesy of the Chi Mei
Museum, Taiwan

ABOVE Amati, Andrea 1570c.

apprenticed to Amati at an early age and learned his trade under Nicolo Amati. Stradivari then went on to experiment with the design and found that by lowering the arching of the violin he was able to produce an instrument that had superior volume and projection, a great necessity of the period as the violin became a solo concert instrument. He was an expert with the knife and cut very fine f-holes.

During his lifetime Stradivari made well over 1,000 instruments – including harps, guitars, violas and cellos – and his innovations and eye for form have never been surpassed. He went on making violins, or at least contributing to their construction, until his death. His sons succeeded him, but they never matched the craftsmanship of their father.

The history of violin making in Cremona, however, really began with the Amati family. Andrea Amati (1525–1611), the father of the family, began as a viol and rebec maker, and went on to make highly decorated, ornate instruments for Charles IX of France. Antonio and Hieronymus Amati (also known as the brothers Amati) were the sons of Andrea Amati. Nicolo Amati (1596–1684), the son of Girolamo Amati, is considered the greatest

RIGHT Antique map of Cremona, Italy. *Steve Estvanik*

instrument maker in the Amati family and was probably the teacher of Stradivari.

Andrea Guarneri (1626–1698), founder of the Guarneri family, was a contemporary apprentice of Stradivari under Nicolo Amati. Giuseppe Guarneri del Gesù (1698–1744) was the most notable of the Guarneri family. The 'del Gesù' part of his name, meaning 'Jesus', was an affectation that he added because his labels were adorned with a little cross and the 'IHS' motif – a Christogram denoting the first three letters of Jesus's name in Greek. He probably made in the region of 200 violins during his life but was shadowed somewhat by his contemporary Stradivari.

In Cremona, where there is still a flourishing violin-making tradition, we also find Carlo Bergonzi (1683–1747), Francesco Ruggieri (c1630–1698), Giovanni Battista Guadagnini (1711–1786) and Lorenzo Storioni (1744–1816).

Florentine schools
Florence, Bologna and Rome may be classed together in a school that dates from around 1680 to 1760, with makers such as Giovanni Gabrielli (1716–1771) and David Tecchler (1666–1748).

Venetian schools
It was natural that the violin-making trade should flourish in Venice owing to the city's position as a trade centre in 18th century Italy combined with the musical innovations of resident composers such as Vivaldi. Venetian violin makers supplied instruments to all walks of life, rich and poor alike, in contrast to the royal patronage of the Cremonese makers.

The Gofriller brothers, Matteo and Francesco, working from around 1700 to 1735, used a characteristic red varnish. Pietro Guarneri (1695–1762), the older brother of del Gesù, moved to Venice from Cremona in the early 18th century. Domenico Montagnana (1686–1750), Francesco Gobetti (1675–1723) and Sanctus Seraphin (1699–1766) were other significant Venetian violin makers.

Tyrolean schools
No evidence exists for any German violin making that was contemporary with da Salo and Maggini, but there were plenty of viol and lute makers at the time, and perhaps some of these dabbled with the violin – but only after the Italian makers had perfected the form.

In the middle of the 17th century manufacture of lutes and viola d'amore was at its peak, the beautiful inlays of pearl and tortoiseshell on these instruments a testament to the skill of the craftsmen working in the region. However, the Tyrolean school never seemed to emerge as great a producer of violins until industrial manufacture of the instrument took hold.

RIGHT AND BELOW Stainer, Jacob 1656.

Courtesy of the Chi Mei Museum, Taiwan

Jacob Stainer (1620–1683), who died a madman and a pauper, was the most celebrated Tyrolean maker and his work remained unsurpassed in the region. Appointed to the Archduke in Austria and later to the court of the Emperor, he received good patronage until the Jesuits accused him of heresy and he was flung in jail, his flourishing career destroyed. Many Stainer instruments have a lion's head in place of the traditional Italian volute at the end of the neck. This was more in keeping with the wood-carving traditions associated with making viola d'amore and viola da gamba instruments, which also featured intricately carved heads.

There were two other interesting makers from the Tyrolean region. Mattias Klotz (1656–1743), thought to have been a pupil of Stainer, was founder of the Mittenwald school of violin making. Mathias Albani (1621–1673) produced work resembling Stainer's designs, but his son, also Mathias, brought in some Italian traits.

French schools

French violin making appears to have begun in the early part of the 17th century. The French were interested in a balance between quantity and quality, most makers content with copying instruments from the Italian schools, notably Brescia and Cremona. The French also tended to use oil-based varnishes less than the Italians, perhaps because the lengthy drying times were not conducive to fast production.

Another obscurity that seems to have emanated from the French schools (and used by English schools) was the practice of baking instruments in an attempt to age the wood for the sake of appearance. Literature tells us that some instruments were baked in sawdust for a week. We cannot imagine what this did to the quality of the instrument apart from drying the wood out further – a kind of forced seasoning.

Nicolas Lupot (1784–1824) is considered by some to be the French Stradivari, his instruments having varnish with marvellous depth and transparency. Interestingly, he left an inscription in a violin about a crack repair he undertook – *retabli*

Courtesy of the Chi Mei Museum, Taiwan

LEFT AND ABOVE Lupot, Nicolas 1799.

Courtesy of the Chi Mei Museum, Taiwan

par Nicolas Lupot, Luthier (restored by Nicolas Lupot, Luthier) – complete with his address.

Jean-Baptiste Vuillaume (1798–1875) was a very fine maker who was also an instrument dealer, a position that gave him the opportunity to copy original violins and create almost exact facsimiles that could be sold for a high price. He experimented scientifically with violins, studying their acoustics and analysing varnishes.

English schools

It is strange that the English school has gone largely undocumented and unnoticed in studies of violin making in the 18th and 19th century, such as the work of Belgian musicologist François-Joseph Fétis. This seems a shame as the English school of violin making has turned out some great instruments – and, admittedly, some real stinkers too. There appear to have been many English makers working independently and producing good instruments.

The English, it seemed, at first preferred the Tyrolean pattern of Stainer, but then moved over to the Italian style in the 18th century. There was an established viol-making craft in England that in all likelihood copied Brescian viols, as indicated by surviving examples. Into the 19th century, unfortunately, English violin makers became unable to compete on price with continental makers and were driven to mass manufacture, the violin being turned into a commodity. Compared with the early makers in Italy, the concept of patronage and aristocratic funding had all but disappeared, replaced by the demand for quantity.

Benjamin Banks (1727–1795), who was based in Salisbury but sold many of his violins at a London dealership, copied from Stainer and then the Amati violin forms. William Forster (1739–1807) was employed in London and then started his own business in the Strand; as was common in the period, there were several William Forsters in the family, all involved in music or instrument making. Alexander Kennedy (1700–1786)

ABOVE Parker, Daniel 1728.

was another London maker who copied the Stainer model, while Barak Norman (1688–1740), originally a lute maker, copied Maggini forms.

BELOW Old violin-maker sign.

Notable bow makers

François Tourte (1747–1835) is credited with the design of the bow as we have it today, evolved from the arched baroque design. He was sought out by Viotti, a contemporary violinist of the day, and with Viotti's ideas and input Tourte made several important modifications to the bow, the most noticeable being the change of the bend from convex to concave.

François Nicolas Voirin (1833–1885), considered to be the Tourte of his day, worked under Vuillaume and eventually established his own business. John Dodd (1752–1839), a contemporary of François Tourte, made fine bows that were a little on the short side. James Tubbs (1835–1921) is considered to have been the 'English Tourte' and produced thousands of bows in his lifetime.

CHAPTER 2

Anatomy of the violin

The violin is a piece of fine woodwork constructed of many components, some of which are designed to be replaceable and adjustable. Quality instruments have their parts and structure precisely fitted for optimal quality of sound production.

How a violin works

Sound is a vibration in a medium detected in humans by highly sensitive detection equipment – our ears. We will consider air as our sound-transmission medium as we have the good fortune to be immersed in a lot of it here on planet Earth. Without air movement, there is no sound, so the violin, like most other Earth-bound instruments, would be useless in the vacuum of space. You could, however, play the violin underwater, but you would probably get some interesting acoustics, and if at sea you might have trouble with the occasional pod of bemused whales.

The violin is a resonator built to respond to a range of frequencies generated by the strings. On its own a taut violin string does not make very much sound because it is too small to move much air around. But when the vibration of the string is channelled through a wooden resonator, the air mass that is moved increases considerably. The resonator both amplifies and filters the string vibration to create a wall of sound. Amplification is achieved because the surface area is larger in proportion to its mass, and the wood of the violin resonates in sympathy with the string. The curvature of the violin surface also helps to increase the amplification of the string vibration, and a note emerges from the silence.

The strings are held taut between the pegs and the tailpiece,

crossing the nut and the bridge. The bridge creates a nodal point, and its position is critical for production of sound. Vibrations from the strings pass down through the bridge and into the violin body. The bridge acts as a filter mixer, mixing four separate vibrations and supplying that to the top plate. Different bridge designs can selectively filter or enhance vibrations of the string. The top plate is thus made to vibrate and the air in the violin body is set in motion.

The sound post channels the vibrations to the back of the violin, and also acts as a pivot point for one of the bridge feet. The other bridge foot is free to move up and down above the position of the bass bar; the bass bar acts as a counterweight to the pulse. The sound reflects off the back of the violin and is forced out through the f-holes, which, combined with the vibration of the front, create the violin's unique sound.

String vibration is induced by plucking or bowing, or some other enterprising method. Bowing is very efficient at creating a continuous vibration, whereas plucking creates a vibration impulse that subsides quickly. The amplitude of vibration is controlled by the size of the pluck or the bowing technique, which includes speed and pressure, as well as position on the string. The frequency of vibration is controlled by the location on the fingerboard of the fingers pressing the string.

Spruce is chosen by violin makers because it is a good resonator, because it has good acoustic properties (ie, sound travels well through the wood) and because it is strong enough to be worked to sufficient thinness. Violins have been made using other materials such as carbonfibre and even glass.

BELOW Bowing is very efficient at creating a continuous vibration.

The parts of the violin

Exterior

Back

The back is commonly made from slow-grown maple, in one or two pieces. Two pieces are preferable for violins, both acoustically and aesthetically. The two-piece back is stronger than the one-piece and can be made thinner as a result. Why is this good? Firstly, the violin is lighter. Secondly, a thinner plate responds better to the vibration induced by the strings, making the violin sing a little better. With a two-piece back, the maker is able to do interesting things with the natural wood pattern (or flame).

Belly (or front)

The belly is usually made from slow-grown and even-grained spruce, chosen for its excellent acoustic properties and strength in the right directions. The front is always a two-piece item, for strength and acoustic design. The belly may also be referred to as the soundboard, top plate, or table in some circles.

Neck, peg box and scroll

The neck, peg box and scroll are carved out of a solid block of maple. Close attention is paid to the direction of the grain, and the quality of the wood, as the neck is under a lot of strain when the strings are on.

Saddle

The saddle is made of ebony, or other hard wood. It supports the tension along the tailpiece and prevents the front from being damaged.

Nut

The nut is normally made of ebony. There are four grooves to ensure proper placement of the strings on and above the fingerboard. When the grooves get too deep, the strings will buzz.

Fingerboard

The fingerboard is usually made of ebony or rosewood, a hard wood to withstand the rigours of play, but some violins have cheaper stained fingerboards or veneered fingerboards. Along its length the fingerboard is concave, which allows the strings to vibrate without buzzing.

Purfling

Purfling is the decorative stripe around the rim of the back and front of the violin. It is normally black and white inlaid wood, but some poor-quality instruments have drawn-on purfling.

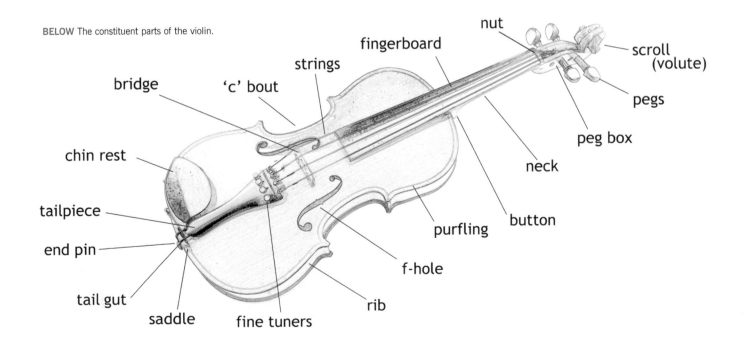

BELOW The constituent parts of the violin.

ANATOMY OF THE VIOLIN

Purfling is more than just a decorative addition to the violin; it provides some protection from cracks that may otherwise spread to the interior of the front or back. It also helps the back and front flex more freely. Purfling ends at the corners in what is termed a 'bee-sting'. Purfling can be made from pear wood, maple, boxwood, beech, poplar, ebony or a fruitwood such as cherry.

The f-holes

The f-holes are decorative features of the front of the violin. The style and placement of f-holes are particular to a maker, and also a mark of the maker's skill with the knife – a nice f-hole will have a good, crisp, clean cut. The f-holes also allow sound to emanate from the violin, and provide a convenient entry point for adjusting the sound post.

Ribs

The ribs are normally made of maple, either plain or with a pleasing flame pattern. On good-quality instruments these are book-matched to form a continuous pattern around the violin. They effectively separate the front and back of the violin and provide the flexibility in the structure of the instrument that is needed to make sound.

Varnish and ground

The finish of the violin is applied in many coats to create the colour. Some makers 'antique' the violin to introduce artificial wear in the varnish. Many makers create their own varnish;

some amateurs have succeeded in setting fire to their houses in doing so.

Although there are hundreds of recipes for varnish, involving various colours and bases, there are two main categories of varnish: oil and spirit. The classic varnish is a combination of linseed oil, resin and turpentine, designed to allow the detail and reflectivity of the wood and ground to show.

Varnishes are variously coloured with lakes, which essentially have miniscule particles of colour suspended in the base varnish. Thus the varnish is both translucent and coloured at the same time, light reflecting off the suspended colour particles but also penetrating to the ground and reflecting back.

Inside the violin

Blocks

The blocks are structural pillars inside the violin around which the ribs adhere and form. There are normally six blocks in good-quality instruments: a top block to which the neck is attached, a bottom block where the end pin goes, and four corner blocks at the points of the C-bouts.

Linings

The linings are found inside the violin, running around the interior ribs of the front and back. They are normally made of willow or spruce and serve to provide a gluing area for the front and back of the violin and to strengthen the ribs. Linings are let in to the blocks on good-quality violins.

Bass bar

The bass bar acts as a pivot inside the violin for the bridge; it also strengthens the front, where the most tension originates from the strings. It is made of spruce, and glued in place on the inside of the front of the violin. The bass bar fit is very accurately made. On some lower-quality violins, the bass bar is instead carved out of the inside of the front.

Sound post

The sound post, found inside the violin, is a dowel of spruce, around 6mm in diameter, connecting the front and back. It is not glued in place and is held in position by the tension of the strings. It is very important for sound production, and helps transmit vibrations created by the strings. The tonal quality and power of a violin can be altered by moving the position of the sound post relative to the bridge. Even a small movement can change the sound for the better, or worse!

Fittings

Bridge

The bridge supports the strings above the front of the violin. Its position is paramount to good sound, and is closely related

RIGHT Tailpieces and adjusters.

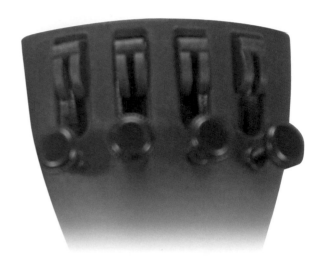

to the position of the bass bar and sound post, the three pieces acting in unison during sound production. The bridge is normally carved from good-quality maple, and may have a style pertaining to a particular maker. They are often stamped with the maker's mark.

Tailpiece

The tailpiece can be made of wood, metal or plastic and serves to hold the strings in place at the bottom of the violin. The tailpiece can be fitted with fine tuners, and some tailpieces can be very ornate. The tailpiece is secured in place by tail gut wrapped around the end pin.

Tail gut

The tail gut is the loop that attaches the tailpiece to the end pin; it provides adjustment of the tailpiece distance.

End pin

The end pin is at the bottom of the violin and the tail gut is attached to it, holding the tailpiece in place. It is made of wood or plastic, and fitted through the bottom rib into the bottom block.

Strings

The strings are the vibrational component of the violin. The vibrations produced by the strings are passed into the body of the violin via the bridge, causing sympathetic resonance of the whole body, and the production of sound.

Different strings will alter the sound of your instrument, and you might want to try different types of string to find the one most suited to your style of playing and the characteristics of the instrument. You can buy gut, synthetic-core or steel strings, all available in different weights. In general, a thick string will give more volume and a thin string will give a brighter sound.

Pegs

The pegs allow the strings to be tuned to pitch. Traditionally they are made of hard wood such as ebony, boxwood or rosewood, but cheaper violins may use plastic. Pegs are fitted precisely to the violin peg box. There are now modern pegs with built-in gears that allow the strings to be tuned accurately without the peg body turning in the peg hole.

BELOW The end pin.

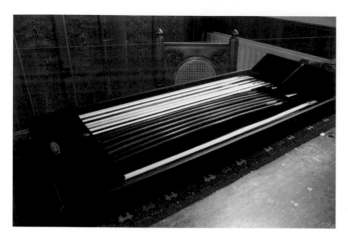

ABOVE Bows in a case.

Bow

The bow has evolved in its own right from a single string on a stick to the elegant French and English styles of the modern bow.

Bow stick

The bow stick is a length of wood with a specially shaped end, which is called the head. The stick is heated and bent into the gentle curve of the bow. For the best durability, the stick should be straight-grained and dense.

Pernambuco is the best wood to use for the bow, but unfortunately it takes a long time to grow, and it is endangered and regulated. Thus supplies of Pernambuco have been reduced and other materials – Brazil wood, cherry wood, snake wood, glassfibre, graphite and carbonfibre to name but a few – have been sought.

Head

The head of the bow is an integral part of the stick, but carved into a beautiful shape. The shape of the head is a characteristic mark of the maker and famous makers such as François Tourte, John Dodd and James Tubbs each have their own trademark pattern.

Bow hair

Good-quality bow hair comes from the horse, the best quality perhaps from the Mongolian horse.

Adjuster (screw and button)

The adjuster is the small screw at the end of the bow that can be turned to move the frog up and down the bow. This action adjusts the tension of the bow hair.

Frog

The frog may be constructed of plastic, ebony, horn or lignum vitae (a dense wood), and finished with nickel or silver fittings. It is attached to the adjuster, and can be moved in order to adjust the tension in the bow hair, which is held in the frog by a mortise.

Rosin

As a player, you rub a little rosin on to the bow hair, and the roughness of the hair helps grip the rosin particles. When the bow is played on the violin strings, the rosin melts under an increase in temperature due to friction, and grips the strings. When the string tension is equal to the grip of the rosin, the string releases and vibrates. This is why your violin gets covered in rosin dust all the time with it being flicked off the string and bow when you play!

Styles of bow

The style of the bow comes in the design of the frog and the head, the choice of lapping, the design of the screw, and the design and finish of the bow stick. The bow stick can be octagonal or circular in cross section, and can have beautiful figure and finish.

The better bows have silver mountings, but nickel is more common. Although you will not find a hallmark on silver bow hardware, you can tell the difference by looking at how the metal has oxidised over time – silver will tarnish black whereas nickel tends to be greenish.

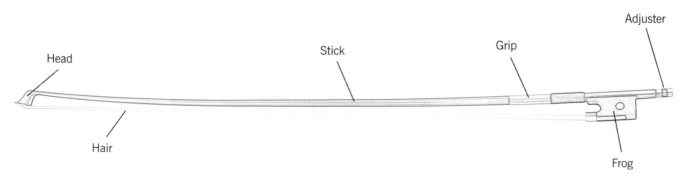

Head

Hair

Stick

Grip

Adjuster

Frog

ABOVE The constituent parts of the bow.

Construction of a violin

Violin construction is a painstaking process and professional violin makers study the art of construction for three to four years before starting in the trade. There are many excellent violin-making schools in the UK, France, Italy, Germany, Switzerland and the USA.

Violin making is a true art form requiring meticulous woodworking skills, taking many years to master and perfect. Each part is fashioned with care and attention to critical measurements, angles and aesthetics. The craft is far from dying and in fact is very much alive and well, the time-honoured skills being passed on to the next generation of makers.

Violin construction usually begins with making templates of the shape of the instrument you wish to emulate. These can be reused every time you want to create a new instrument based on the pattern. There are some makers who strike out on their own, and others who create their own pattern templates from scratch using mathematical principles; for the adventurous there are one or two good books on this process (see 'Further reading and resources').

Everything from the silhouette outline of the instrument to the intricacies of the scroll can be expressed in mathematical terms,

ABOVE Making a violin.

and then used to create an instrument. It is not surprising that this is so, as the violin was developed at a time when renewed thinking about mathematics and geometry was flourishing. You may come across terms such as the Golden Ratio and Fibonacci Sequence describing mystical relationships between numbers and proportion. These principles were applied to the design of the violin scroll volute, and also to the ratios and proportions of the violin body. The volute spiral, a beautiful pattern, is widely found in nature, from the unfurling of a fern leaf to the spiral of a nautilus.

BELOW Spiral in a nautilus. *Joingate*

BELOW Spiral in a fern. *Marc Parsons*

So we can thank Nature herself for the appealing form of the violin, for it was she who inspired the great thinkers and designers of the time.

The body template of the violin defines the silhouette of the instrument. Normally there will be an inside and an outside template: the inside template defines the line of the ribs; the outside template defines the overhang over the ribs.

From the template, a 'mould' can be fashioned. Most modern makers use an interior mould, the violin being constructed around it. The mould is usually made of solid wood, with holes drilled for clamping ribs and blocks. Other forms of making use exterior moulds or no mould at all, but for consistent results interior mould construction is considered the norm.

Blocks are fashioned from good-quality spruce or sometimes willow, shaped and glued into place on the mould. Throughout the process animal glue is used so that everything is reversible and adjustable; relatively weak animal glue is used to secure the blocks, as the mould will be disengaged later during the construction process.

There are normally six blocks – a top block, a bottom block and four corner blocks – but some older and poorly made violins do not have six blocks. If you remove the end pin and look into the interior of the violin you will be able to see the blocks. The blocks are shaped to the inside template, for it is these that will support the rib structure of the instrument.

The ribs are prepared and formed next around the outside of the mould, and carefully steam-bent to create the graceful curves of the violin. Ribs must be thinned to around 1mm to allow them to be bent easily and flex properly when the violin is played. The surfaces of the ribs are initially planed and then carefully scraped smooth to bring out the pattern in the wood. Ribs can be highly figured but, as every violin maker knows, these are the most difficult to work with, the wood tending to tear out and split as they are prepared. With beauty comes a price, as an old violin master maker once said.

Willow or spruce linings are glued inside the

rims of the ribs to reinforce them and provide a gluing surface for the front and back. These are carefully thinned down and let into the blocks of the violin. 'Letting' – the word used to describe how the linings are inset into the blocks – provides strength and a rigid anchor point, and is a sign of a well-made violin. Linings are glued on both the top and bottom of the ribs, for the back and front of the instrument – which may beg the question to how the mould is removed.

ABOVE Blocks and ribs.

Usually the ribs are left on the mould until just before the violin front and back are to be glued. This is because the ribs may have the tendency to warp without the support, the whole thing becoming very un-violin-shaped after a short while. To

BELOW Interior view: an end block and linings.

disengage the mould from the ribs, the violin maker pops the blocks off the mould with a sharp tap of a hammer, and then carefully bends out the sides of the violin to allow the mould to drop out. There is enough flexibility in the violin ribs to allow this, and the linings support the rib during this slightly unnerving process.

The front is fashioned from a wedge of spruce, the back from a wedge of maple, arched and hollowed following precise thickness patterns. The wedge is created from quarter-sawn wood, although sometimes a solid back can be found. Two pieces of quarter-sawn wood are glued side by side to create a squashed diamond shape in profile. The join between these two pieces of wood must be as near to perfect as can be made, this forming the centreline of the violin front or back. This is the feared and respected centre join, which, to get right, may take from a few hours to a few days for the uninitiated.

Next the wedge is planed flat on one side, and the structure of the ribs used to define the outline of the violin, centred on the centre join. The violin front is then arched using some profile templates to define the height and curvature of the arching; this is usually done with a gouge initially, followed by thumb planes and finally scrapers to achieve the profile. The whole thing is flipped over and gouged out, until the desired thickness of the violin is achieved; the thickness varies over the surface of the front.

BELOW Modes of vibration.

Some makers will listen to the tone of the wood as the gouging process takes place by a process called tap toning. The wood begins to ring as it loses some of its thickness and gains flexibility. During the process standing waves can be set up in the wood by tapping at particular spots on the surface. There are optimal tap tones for the front and back, corresponding to the required vibrational modes needed to produce good music within the range of the violin.

The vibrational patterns can also be seen using what is technically termed as loose-leaf tea, which can be sprinkled on the violin front. When the violin front is excited by means of a loud frequency generator, the tea will migrate to the nodes of vibration, forming a pattern on the violin surface. The patterns of vibration are most distinct at the resonance of the surface with the driving frequency. The brand of loose-leaf tea used appears not to matter much, although store own brands are recommended because they are cheaper!

Purfling is laid into the front and back around the edge. A channel is cut using a purfling cutter, and the thin strips of pear wood carefully laid in sections. As Stradivari once did, the best makers are able to create bee-sting details at the corners, where the purfling edges meet. Often a close look at the violin purfling will give some indication of the skill of the maker. Is the channel cleanly cut? Is the purfling crisp and even?

The f-holes are cut following pattern templates and precise positioning to give a good aesthetic to the violin. The f-hole is particular to the maker and varies in appearance; some are

slender, some are fat, some are regal, and some are plain. They are all part of what gives the instrument its character, and again the mark of a good maker is the precision and placement of the f-holes.

A bass bar is fashioned from spruce and glued into the interior of the front. The position and fit of the bass bar is critical to the quality and sound of the violin.

The neck and scroll is carved from a piece of solid maple following a pattern template. The scroll forms a beautiful three-dimensional volute.

The front and back are glued to the rib structure, and the neck mortised into the top block at the correct angle. This

essentially finishes the instrument 'in the white'. It can then be finished with fine, abrasive fish scale or horse tail, and thoroughly cleaned in preparation for fitting up and varnishing.

BELOW A violin 'in the white'.

BELOW Chopping out a peg box.

Cousins of the modern violin

In your travels you may hear described or see instruments that are almost like a modern violin but differ in some very specific ways. We present a brief description of these instruments so that you may recognise them.

Baroque violins

'Baroque' is the term given to violins that are built and set up for

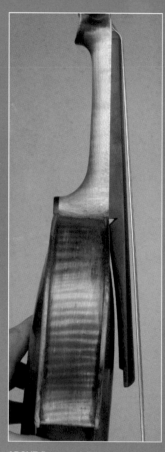

ABOVE Baroque violin neck angle, *Anoixe*

baroque playing. The sound of a baroque set-up is quite different from the familiar modern sound, its lower volume more attuned to chamber music than full orchestral recitals. Some regard baroque sound as insipid and feeble, but others describe it as mellow and rich with overtones. We leave readers to come to their own conclusions about the instrument and the music – 'baroque and roll'.

A baroque violin is strung with gut and the bridge is lower, more gently arched and thicker at the top – but considerable variation is found. The neck runs parallel to the plates (the modern neck is angled backwards) and is also markedly shorter, and thus the instrument does not have the range of a modern violin. The bass bar is generally smaller in a baroque violin, and the bow is convex instead of the modern concave design.

ABOVE AND BELOW Hardanger fiddle. *Bevan Wulfenstein, Wulffenstejn Hardanger Fiddle & Mandolin Works*

Hardanger fiddles

Probably originating in the region of the Hardanger fjord in Norway, Hardanger fiddles – *Hardingfele* in Norwegian – are very interesting instruments, their peculiar difference being an extra set of sympathetic strings that run through the bridge under the primary strings and along the underside of the fingerboard. The effect of these strings is to produce a sympathetic droning sound when the fiddle is played. It is thought that this idea evolved from the viola d'amore design and certainly there are similarities.

The fingerboard and fittings are richly inlaid with pearl and ivory or bone. The fiddles are inked (rosed) on the sides and back with intricate designs. The scroll is a Norwegian lion, which looks like a Viking ship's prow topped with a crown. There can be four or five sympathetic strings and they are tuned in a particular way.

Hardanger instruments are made with spruce for the front and maple – or sometimes alder – for the back. A Hardanger shares the violin bass bar and much of the construction is the same as a modern violin, but the f-holes are cut very differently. Owing to the higher arch needed for the sympathetic strings, the cutting of the f-hole begins while the front is still being hollowed out at the back. The fingerboard, which is often spruce with an ebony veneer, is much flatter than that of a violin and has a gentler radius. A Hardanger bridge is also very different, being higher, flatter across the top, and with holes for the sympathetic strings that pass under the main strings. Overall, the amount of variation in construction and style can be considerable.

Today there are a few Hardanger makers in Scandinavia as well as the UK and the US. Although gaining in popularity, the instruments have a relatively small following, and part of the problem is the very limited availability of design material for making a Hardanger. Sverre Sandvik wrote a book, *Vi Byggjer Hardingfele*, that is now out of print and quite impossible to find – the authors took over a year to secure a copy through professional book hunters! Furthermore, the entire book is in Norwegian, but, critically, the plans in the back provide the important measurements required to make a Hardanger. There is an English translation available by Eldon Ellingson, but this is just as hard to come by and the translation is not very accurate. Unlike the violin market, there are no mass-produced Hardanger instruments available for beginners at an affordable price. There are also no published auction prices for Hardanger fiddles.

The reason why the Hardanger is less known today is that mass-produced imported violins became increasingly available in Norway in the 18th and 19th centuries and players there gradually adopted these. Perhaps the *Hardingfele* craft would have disappeared into obscurity entirely had there not been a well-established folk tradition, since there was no reason to have a centre of violin making in Norway with the deluge of European trade instruments. But survive it did, and we can but hope for its popularity to increase as more people experience the ethereal tones of the *Hardingfele*.

So if you come across a violin with rich inlay, rosing, an unusual-looking scroll and more strings than you think it should have, you may well have a Hardanger in your hands!

Viola d'amore

The viola d'amore, a predecessor of the violin but quite different from it, appeared in Europe during the 17th century. The instrument has seven playing strings and sympathetic strings were common, with seven strings passing under the fingerboard. Like the Hardanger fiddle, the strings produce a characteristic droning sound, and make for a very long peg box! It is common

ABOVE A Viola D'Amore, and a practice Viola D'Amore, *Bevan Wulfenstein, Alma Jay Young, Hardingfele.com*

for the f-holes to be carved in the form of an Islamic flame, which provides a clue to the origins of this instrument in the Arab world. The back is generally flat, the instrument features deep ribs, and instead of a scroll it may have an intricately carved blind cupid.

Some violin makers also made viola d'amore, and Storioni is a good example of a maker who combined features of the two instruments. Until very recently it was possible to study the making of a Storioni viola d'amore at the Newark School of Violin Making.

Electric violins

Working on the same principle as the electric guitar, the electric violin relies on magnetic pickups to convert metal string vibrations into electric signals. The signals are then amplified and modified to create the sound. Because an electric violin does not rely on air mass movement, it can be made in more eclectic forms than a traditional acoustic violin.

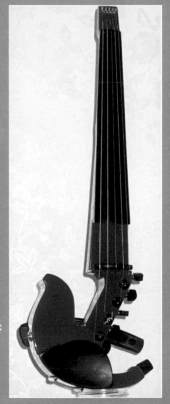

The sound of an electric violin is familiar yet different. There may be more strings than the traditional four, sometimes up to seven, and therefore the playing style can differ. In fact there are musical works composed entirely for six-stringed electric violins.

The electric violin has one benefit over all others: it can be played in silence so that only the player can hear it through headphones, making it a fantastic practice violin!

RIGHT An electric violin, *Just plain bill*

Accessories

Shoulder rest

There are two commonly found main types of shoulder rest – Kun and Wolf – and these are recommended because they are adjustable. The padded part can be individually bent to the shoulder of the player and, correctly fitted, the shoulder rest should look like a smiley face – if it is unhappy you have it on the wrong way!

Other kinds of shoulder rest are becoming available. One, developed by the Alexander family, is designed so that you do not have to change your posture and cause stress to your shoulder and neck. This is especially good for a player who practises for many hours every day.

It may take a while to find the design that best suits you, and the thing to do is try out various types if you can. You may end up purchasing a few different designs, and as a player you may like to vary the use of shoulder rests so you can appreciate the differences between them.

Chin rest

There are two main types of chin rest. The more popular, and preferable, type is the Guarneri chin rest, which sits over the button and tailpiece. This is good because there is always a danger that an unwary player may over-tighten the clamp. As a Guarneri chin rest clamps on to the bottom block of the violin, damage through accidental over-tightening is less likely.

The other popular kind of chin rest called a Kaufman chin rest is flat and shallow and can cause bulging on the bottom rib

BELOW Guarneri chin rest.

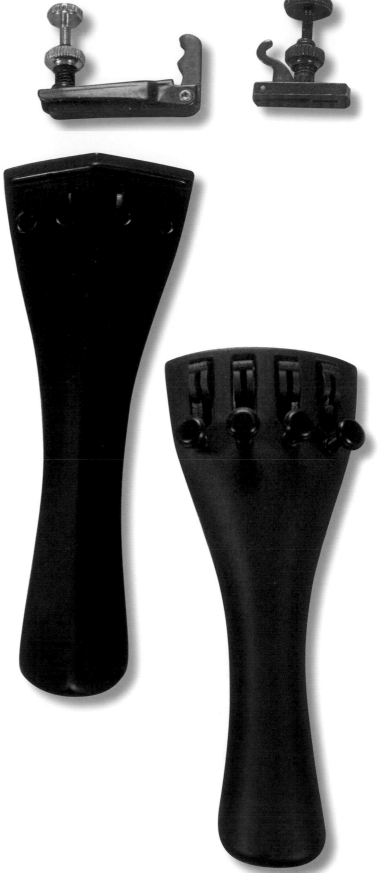

on the bass side, or in severe cases it can actually crack the rib if over-tightened. Another potential pitfall is that the adjustment keyhole can go all the way through the rest, so that the key, if inserted too far, can scratch the varnish when turned. Be aware of this one! One other piece of advice – put the key on a key ring as it is very easy to lose.

Chin rests are normally lined with cork to protect the instrument. The problem with this is that over the years the cork sticks and, when you finally come to change the chin rest, the cork stays behind on the instrument. If this happens there is no need to panic: just try a little bit of water to soak it off, having first put a tiny cotton bud of water on a test piece to make sure that the varnish does not react. If the test provides the necessary reassurance, get some tissue, soak it in water and lay it over the cork until suitably dampened. The cork should gently come away; if you have to pull too hard it could take varnish off, so let it soak for a while longer if it does not come off straight away.

Tailpiece

Tailpieces come in different materials, and this is perhaps one of those instances where plastic is better than the wood and metal alternatives. Wooden tailpieces look nicer, but the built-in adjusters do not have as much range as the plastic ones. Metal is the least favourite, as it can sometimes produce a metallic buzz when the violin is played.

Tailpieces also come in different styles: tulip-shaped, French and Hill patterns. The Hill pattern has a ridge running down the centre and is quite distinct.

Some players may prefer to have only the E and A strings with fine adjusters, in which case a wooden tailpiece is fine. A tailpiece in a nice ebony, boxwood or rosewood looks good, and if you use boxwood do have the chin rest in the same wood so all fittings match.

If you use a plastic tailpiece with built-in adjuster we recommend you use the Wittner version with pegs and chin rest in ebony to keep everything matching nicely.

Wolf note eliminator

A wolf note is an unintended sound that emanates from the instrument in sympathy with another note. It can sound quite out of place and happens because there are innate resonances between the instrument and strings that are excited during play. Wolf notes are more common on cellos than on violins and violas.

A wolf note eliminator is a weight that is attached to the string. It comes in a tube with a rubber sleeve inside, and this sleeve is fitted on the offending string between the bridge and

tailpiece. The metal case is attached over it with the locking screw. This device has the effect of moving the wolf note to a useful tone, which may not sound at all.

Some players actually like to have a wolf note. This does not mean that the instrument is any better or worse – it is just part of the instrument's character.

Dampener

A dampener is used to increase the humidity inside an instrument and is only really needed in more extreme environments. As wood responds to changes in environment, it can be useful to stabilise it, especially in very dry conditions.

A dampener is a plastic rubber tube with holes in it and a wick inside. When placed in a source of water outside the instrument, the wick absorbs moisture and thereby provides a little bit of humidity inside the instrument.

Mute

A mute is used to quieten the output of your instrument and allow practice without disturbing other people, or yourself, especially when learning to play the violin. It is like a comb that slides on to the bridge and stops the strings from being so loud.

The most common type of mute is made of rubber. It slides on to the A and D strings, and has a little groove that fits over the bridge. It can be easily turned on and off to unlock the full volume of the instrument.

Over the years there have been some fancy designs of mute in silver, gold and ivory, as well as combinations of metals and materials such as silver and tortoiseshell.

Case

It is sensible to invest in a good case to protect your instrument. In your travels you may see several different designs of varying practicality.

Early cases were made of wood and were coffin-shaped, and are often seen in antique shops. Avoid buying an old case such as this, as you may be buying 'bow bug' as well (see Chapter 5, 'Basic maintenance'). It is preferable to invest in a modern case.

Styrofoam cases should be avoided. Although they are light and good at cushioning, they can also be trouble because Styrofoam is too soft – you can push your finger into it – and does not have much strength. We have seen circumstances where a Styrofoam case looked sound but the instrument inside was crushed.

The better cases to go for are the somewhat heavier designs that are carbonfibre-reinforced on the outside and trimmed on the inside in a lighter material. A hard shell case is so much better because it is your first line of defence when the knocks and bangs come, and they will come! It is a good idea to compare the weight of different cases before making your choice, because you will be the one carrying it around.

A case normally has a secure place for bows. It is a good idea to check the fit of your violin and accessories in the case before purchase.

One last tip is to put a belt or strap around the case when travelling; this is an extra precaution just in case the catches give way at an inopportune moment.

Pickups and microphones

If you wish to amplify or record your acoustic violin or do interesting things with the sound on a computer, you can buy a pickup or a microphone. These convert the vibration from the violin into an electrical signal that can then be processed, stored, manipulated, analysed and mangled as you see fit. A violin can be made to sound as if it is being played in an entirely different acoustic environment. By using reverb and echo you can make the violin sound as if it is being played in a large concert hall or a basilica.

Piezo electric transducers are neat little things that produce electrical signals when physically deformed, by sound vibrations, or can be driven with an electrical signal to produce sound. They are the basis of many of the violin pickups that you can buy. Some are fitted into the bridge, some clamp on to the bridge, and some wrap around the violin body.

More traditional microphones work by changing air vibration into electrical signal rather than the surface-mounted piezo transducers. There are microphone mounts for the violin that attach to the tailpiece and allow positioning of the microphone by a flexible gooseneck. This is actually better

ABOVE AND RIGHT A nice Hill case complete with the manufacturer's plate.

if you are trying to capture some nuance as it is adjustable in space around your violin body, whereas a piezo element will be in a fixed position.

Of course you could just buy a standard microphone and record the violin in situ. However, you will get a lot of the room acoustics in the recording as well and you may not want this. Close 'miking' via a mounted microphone or a piezo element will give you more or less complete isolation from other sound sources in the vicinity. If you are interested in miking up, we encourage you to try out a few options!

There are numerous software applications for PC and Mac computers that give you the facilities to capture and play with the sound from your instrument. The authors prefer PCs for their inherent configurable nature. Free applications such as Audacity are readily downloadable from the web. For the more adventurous, applications such as Cakewalk Sonar and Adobe Sound Booth allow real-time manipulation of the sound sources. We recommend a decent sound card if you want to capture good-quality sound; the standard 16-bit sound cards are relatively noisy beasts and are surpassed by the better-quality 24-bit cards produced by companies such as M-Audio.

W. E. HILL & SONS,
Violin Makers,
140, NEW BOND STREET, LONDON, W.

CHAPTER 3

Tools, equipment and materials

Old tools are a pleasure to use because they are generally made of good-quality cast steel and they have history, perhaps indicated by owner stamps on the handles. When buying old tools the thing to watch out for is that the steel is not pitted; a bit of surface rust does not really matter and can be removed with wire wool and elbow grease, but pitting can take hours of work to flatten to an acceptable standard. The tool manufacturers to look for include Addis, Ward, Marples, Sorby, Herring brothers and Howarth.

A few modern companies – Veritas and Lie-Nielsen are examples – make excellent tools of good-quality steel.

LEFT Tool handles displaying their lovely patina.

Tools in detail

Chisels

Chisels are widely used in violin making, from squaring off blocks to making a purfling platform. Chisels come in all shapes and sizes:

- **Bevel chisels** are made so that they are easy to get into tight corners; the bevel runs along the shank.
- **Firmer chisels** are strong and can be used for heavier work; the blade has a rectangular cross section.
- **Paring chisels** are long, thin chisels.
- **Japanese chisels** are made with good steel and sharpen quickly because they are designed with a small hollow on the back of the blade, so less metal needs to be removed when flattening the back near the edge.

The angle of the bevel of the chisel is important. Steeply angled bevels are more suited to heavy work, as the blade is reinforced. A bevel with a lower angle is more like a knife and more precision is possible, but the edge is more vulnerable as there is less metal supporting it.

Gouges

Gouges are used for making scoop cuts from wood, typically for hollowing out fronts and backs, and in the fine carving of the scroll. You can find gouges at antique fairs and sales and it is satisfying to collect them.

There are two main types of gouge of interest to the violin maker:

- **In-canal gouge** – the bevel is on the top side of the gouge; useful for cutting nice curves in corner blocks.

BELOW Gouges.

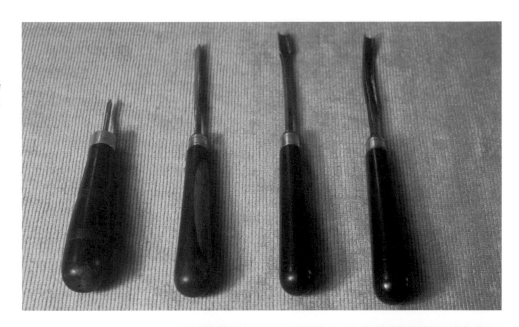

■ **Standard bench gouge** – the bevel is on the outside of the gouge; useful for hollowing out fronts and backs.

Within these two categories there are different sweeps, from V-shaped gouges to gently curving gouges.

There are other specialist gouges used for turning and carving wood that are rarely used in violin repair.

Planes

Planes come in all shapes and sizes, from the tiny thumb planes not much bigger than a fingernail to large smoothing planes longer than your arm. The low-angle block plane, as made by Veritas or Lie-Nielsen, is one of the most useful, but these are not cheap – buy an old one if possible.

Planes with wide mouths are more suited for use on soft woods because the blade does not clog as easily. Planes with thin mouths are better for hard woods and stop the wood tearing up. Some planes have adjustable mouths to accommodate both. You can also buy specialist planes such as toothed versions, which are designed to stop wood tearing out.

BELOW A variety of planes. RIGHT Probably the biggest plane you will ever see.

Knives

A good violin maker's knife – Japanese knives are very good – is invaluable for accurately trimming wood and for cutting f-holes.

Scrapers

Cabinet scrapers are always handy for cleaning up a surface, removing plane marks and general finishing. You can make smaller scrapers from thin spring steel for scraping filler varnish, but you should never scrape off original varnish. A bendy old rule can also be made into a scraper.

Burnisher

A burnisher, normally a piece of hard steel similar to a knife sharpener, is needed to sharpen scrapers. Veritas sell burnishers that make the sharpening process easier.

Rasps and files

Grobet make really good rasps and files that will last and last. If one gets clogged with wood, plunge the file into a container of boiling water, which will expand the metal and cause the wood particles to be released. When you remove the file, the water will evaporate off into steam and you can help this along with a hairdryer on its hottest setting, as you need to get the water dried off before it does it any damage. You can also rub a file with a wire brush or an old toothbrush to loosen stubborn particles.

Needle files are tiny, round files for making grooves on the bridge and nut, and a knife-cut file is also useful for the grooves.

Saws

Japanese saws are marvels of technology. They cut by drawing the saw backwards through the wood, whereas the saws we are used to in the West cut on the forward stroke. A consequence of this design is that the saw can be made much more thinly, as it does not need much support on the saw blade; Western saws use thicker saw blades to resist the tendency to buckle as the saw is pushed through the wood. Japanese saws come in all sizes, for rapid cutting of large pieces of wood to fine work. The fine saws are so good, in fact, that the sawed surface often needs no further preparation.

A fret saw is needed for fine work, where you find yourself cutting curves. When cutting larger areas a coping saw is useful; you will probably need one if making acrylic templates.

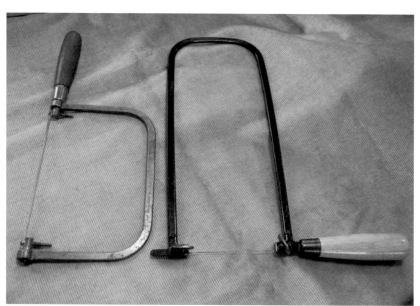

LEFT Coping saw and fret saw.

BELOW Two types of saw.

Template tools

Templates are printed in the back of this book so that you can make template tools at home. Template tools are used when you need a guide or have a specific task that requires a tool that you cannot readily buy and therefore need to design and make yourself. Some specialised violin-making tool shops may sell such items, but it is far cheaper and more satisfying to make your own.

ABOVE AND BELOW Bridge templates.

BELOW Fingerboard curvature templates.

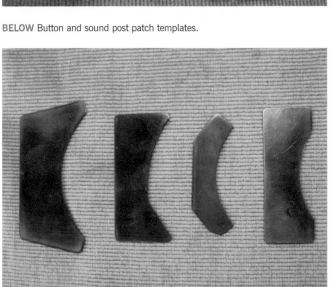

BELOW Button and sound post patch templates.

BELOW Using a button template.

Sharpening stones

You will need sharpening stones and slip stones. In case you are not familiar with a slip stone, this is just a sharpening stone with a curved (concave or convex) edge used for sharpening gouges. For sharpening stones we recommend a coarse diamond stone and a medium and fine Japanese water stone, and for slip stones we recommend a medium and a fine stone.

It is very important to have flat sharpening stones, otherwise you will cause more problems than you fix. To flatten the stones, use wet-and-dry abrasive paper on a good flat surface.

Clamps

You can never have enough clamps and they come in all shapes and sizes. We recommend a good set of G-clamps, some small brass clamps and, if you can get them, some repairers' clamps; Companion Tools make nice repairer clamps. If you can also obtain some stretcher clamps, these will also be useful for crack work.

Closing clamps

At some point you will need some closing clamps. If you want to make your own, you can buy some threaded rod and construct clamps with wooden discs covered in cork or leather to stop them damaging the instrument; the discs are tightened down the rod with a wingnut. But our advice is to buy closing clamps: the best are the Herdim brand but you can buy cheaper Chinese versions on eBay.

A useful repair accessory is some clear acrylic, which helps to apply more even pressure to surfaces under clamps and it bends rather more nicely than the alternative Perspex.

Gluing tools

Violin makers use all sorts of things for warming glue, from

BELOW Bending iron.

baby-bottle warmers to little hot plates, and you can also buy professional glue-pot warmers. We prefer to use a little hot plate with a saucepan full of hot water in which a jam jar of glue is immersed. Baby-bottle warmers tend to get messy quickly and are difficult to clean out.

You need some different-sized brushes of good quality to apply glue. Do not buy cheap brushes because bristles will come out and stick where you do not want them.

Bending irons and bending straps

For replacing a rib or lining it is useful to have a bending iron, a piece of kit that will allow you to steam-bend wood. Not all bending irons are created equal – some are poorly made and the element can burn out after a short period of use. Some violin makers use a blowtorch and a piece of pipe as a crude bending iron.

The bending strap is used to support the wood when it is bent around the iron. The wood is normally dampened first and then moulded into shape with a hot iron.

Specialist tools

The following two specialist tools are unique to violin making:

- **Peg reamer** For reaming out end pin holes and peg holes.
- **Sound post setter** Used for manipulating the sound post inside the violin.

Measuring tools

These are three types of measuring tool that will be useful:

- **Callipers** Used for measuring thicknesses accurately; plastic ones are good because there is little danger of them marking the wood.
- **Set square** Always useful for squaring off pieces of wood and checking if the pieces are square in the first place.
- **Flexible rule** You can buy nice flexible steel rules that are able to measure over the gentle curves of violins.

Miscellaneous equipment

The following items are useful to the violin repairer:

- **Loupe or magnifying glass** Go for one with 5–10 times magnification.
- **Angle-poise lamp** You need a good lamp and an angle-poise type is best as it can be positioned well to highlight wood surfaces and illuminate dark and gloomy places inside the violin.

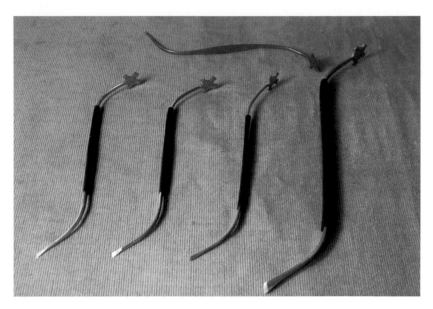

ABOVE Sound post setters.

- **'Bendy' light** This is useful to get light inside the violin when you need to inspect the interior.
- **Dentist's mirror** This is ideal for looking inside a violin via the f-hole. You might find a few surprises – love poems have been found written inside violins!
- **Straight edge** This is a machined precision edge that is guaranteed to be flat within 0.001mm. If you want to ensure something is totally flat, one of these is essential in the workshop.
- **Propelling pencil** The best size is 0.5mm.
- **Dustpan, brush and broom** It goes without saying that you will need to clear up afterwards – it is surprising how much debris you can produce from a little bit of planing.

Miscellaneous consumables

Here are a few other useful items:

- **Fine wire wool** For light abrasion of surfaces.
- **Wet-and-dry abrasive paper** Used for a number of different tasks, so a selection of grits will always come in useful.
- **Methylated spirit** For opening glued surfaces and cleaning things.
- **Lint-free cloth** For wiping up and applying. If you are using certain chemicals (such as linseed oil) be aware that they can combust spontaneously if left on a rag, so a metal waste bin away from flammable objects is a very sensible idea.
- **Chalk** Soft chalk is used for the bridge and sound post or for doing any fitting. Use dressmakers' chalk rather than blackboard chalk, which is too hard. Also be aware chalk will act as a light abrasive if you rub surfaces with it.

Workshop equipment

Benches

Having at least one bench is a good idea, but having more is even better. For luxury you could have the following:

■ **Sharpening bench** Where you can keep all your sharpening stones and grinders; the sharpening process can be messy, so it is a good idea to keep that away from your nice clean woodwork.
■ **Workbench** A good sturdy workbench is a must. You will want it to be heavy and resist movement and vibration: if you are sawing bits of wood or chiselling things, you do not want your work surface wobbling around underneath you like a huge tub of lard. It will result in poor work, and may be hazardous to you. To your workbench you attach your vice with sturdy bolts. The surface of the workbench should be nice and flat and hard-wearing.
■ **Varnishing bench** Where you can do varnishing and retouching of varnish. This does not have to be as heavy-duty as your main workbench, but it should still be sturdy and wobble-free. You may also want to do gluing work here and anything involving chemicals.

Bench vice

Older bench vices are usually more pleasing to use so it is best to look around car boot sales and antique fairs to find a satisfactory one. When you arrive home, strip down the vice and give it a good clean. You can use wire wool to clear light rust, but avoid greasing the vice – and you certainly do not want to cover it in oil. Oil and grease attract dust from your work and threads quickly clog up, so just use a little petroleum jelly or dry soap on the threads. If the vice has wooden blocks on it, you should remove these and change them as you do not know what the wood has been in contact with and what has seeped into it, ready to ooze out and spoil your work. Try to get a bench vice with a quick-release lever.

If you want a new vice, Record make good models but due to their weight they cost a fortune to ship if you buy online.

Power tools

If you are seriously thinking of setting up a workshop you may want to invest in some good labour-saving devices.

Bench grinder

The bench grinder is used for shaping metal and grinding edges. It is invaluable if you want to shape a new knife, grind a badly worn chisel to a new edge, or reshape a plane blade.

Grinders come with different speeds, and with different coarseness and stone abrasive quality depending on the work in hand. Grinding wheels may also come with some nice 'rests' for supporting the blade as you work and help keep it at the correct angle.

The kind of grinders you get in the DIY stores tend to be very aggressive and will remove metal (and anything else actually) at an alarming rate, accompanied by a shower of sparks or organic material if you put your fingers there. So we must emphasise safety when using any power tool.

Always wear safety goggles when using a grinder. Never wear gloves or dangling jewellery, both of which can get stuck in the wheel and cause a nasty accident. Keep hair tied back if you are lucky enough to have hair. When using the grinding wheel, the metal will heat up quite quickly, so be careful not to touch the bit you have just been grinding. Some people use a water bath to cool the metal, and some just allow it to cool naturally. Suffice it to say, do not put hot metal near anything flammable.

When grinding you must not burn the metal, something that can happen readily when working on thin edges. You can tell if you have burned the metal because it goes black or brown and then flakes off – it is then useless as a cutting edge. If you are working on thin edges, you should do so on a water stone grinder or on the sharpening stones. A water stone grinder, which is less scary and will not burn the metal, slowly rotates a grinding stone through a water bath, and it is generally used at the end of the grinding and shaping process.

A manual bench grinder, with a little handle that is geared up to turn a wheel, is another variation that is useful in its own right.

Pillar drill

The pillar drill, also known as a drill press, is used for drilling holes accurately and vertically in materials. If you try to drill vertical holes with a hand drill you often find that the hole profile is not entirely vertical, and this can be critical if you are making a template that requires precise alignment.

Band saw

Used for cutting wood accurately and cleanly, a band saw is capable of making irregular or curved cuts in wood. It can even be used to cut metal if so required. Band saws range from table-top size – ideal if you are limited on space – to large floor-mounted leviathans. The better band saws have a platform that can be tilted for cuts of different angles.

The tightness of a curved cut is dependent on the width of the blade used in the band saw. All band saws have replaceable blades and accept blades of different width and toothed blades for various tasks. Wider blades are less likely to break.

Tool storage

You need to keep your tools in order and if you have invested a lot of money on a range of satisfying hand tools you will want to look after them well. We highly recommend a tool board and shelving.

A tool board is a large board secured firmly to the wall and fitted with pegs and hangers for tools; it may also have a wood block with holes bored in it to store chisels and gouges. Each tool has its place on the tool board and an outline or label shows the location of the tool. In this way you can easily see if you have neglected to put something away, lost something, or something needs replacing because you threw it out.

Tool rolls are useful to keep things tidily together, especially files and rasps but also chisels and gouges. It is wise to keep these sharp tools separate from other tools because they will blunt and quickly become useless if you chuck them all loose in a bag together.

To protect your expensive planes, we recommend plane socks, which cushion the base of the plane against any knocks. We actually use old socks for this purpose and they seem to do the job quite well.

ABOVE Band saw.

Buying tools

A warning: once you start buying tools, it can be difficult to stop. Older tools and well-made modern tools all have their own beauty and form, and older tools have a certain patina that is rare in modern tools. An owner sometimes stamped his name into the handle and it is pleasing to think that a tool is passed on from generation to generation. Older tools also tend to be made of better steel that keeps its edge well. We recommend looking around antique shops, car boot sales and jumble sales as good sources of older second-hand tools.

If a tool has been blunted or the edge nicked, is rusty and uncared for, or the handle is damaged, it is a pleasure to bring it back to life. Rust can be removed, blunted edges can be reprofiled and sharpened, and handles can be replaced. Avoid tools that are heavily pitted: you may not be able to see the real condition of the tool until the rust and grime are removed, so sometimes you just take a chance.

Restoring tools

Here are some simple steps to restore a rusty old chisel to its prime. We hope this whets your appetite.

- Spray some WD40 on to the steel.
- Acquire a kitchen scouring pad.
- Don some surgical gloves.
- Put down some newspaper, or find a place to work where the mess will go unnoticed.

- Scrub the tool with the scouring pad – the rust will flake off. If you do not have much luck, try wire wool.
- Once the rust is removed, you will see the true beauty of the metal shining through.
- You need to decide if the tool needs to be reground or just worked on the coarse sharpening stone. If the edge is completely rounded or badly nicked, you will want to regrind the bevel of the tool and reshape it.

Sharpening tools

Sharpening chisels

There have been entire books about sharpening, and the methods and techniques depend on the tools you are working with. A good tool to learn to sharpen is the chisel, which is used extensively in making and repairing fine woodwork. Here are some tips on how you should sharpen chisels.

You will need some sharpening stones: we recommend diamond stones and Japanese water stones as these cut the metal efficiently and give fast results. Another benefit is that they only require water as the lubricant, and thus the procedure is less messy than working with oil stones. Oil tends to get everywhere, including on your work as it penetrates your hands. Water washes off!

Before you begin, check that your water stones are flat, with a straight edge. If they are not flat you will encounter problems. If they are brand new, then they are likely to be flat, but check them anyway. If they have been used and not flattened in a while, then they are likely to be concave. The only problem with water stones is that they erode quickly (unlike diamond stones), but thankfully it is fairly easy to flatten a worn water stone.

These are the stages of the sharpening procedure:

- **Coarse diamond stone** If the edge is badly blunted, this is used to start the sharpening process and define the edge.
- **Medium water stone** To continue the sharpening process, use this to bring the edge up to sharpness.
- **Fine water stone** This next stage will put a nice polish on to the edge and make it razor-sharp.

- **Leather strop and jeweller's rouge** Used to complete the process and remove any tiny burrs.

Sharpening scrapers

Steel scrapers are used for final finishing of surfaces. They achieve this by a small sharp burr that acts like a miniature plane blade. When you draw a scraper across the surface of wood, a fine shaving is removed if the scraper is properly sharp. If you just get dust or nothing happens, you have a blunt scraper.

To begin you must achieve a nice crisp profile to the steel. The edge of the scraper can be drawn over a file, or coarse sharpening stone, with the scraper held square. We recommend files, because you will end up with grooves in your sharpening stone. Once you have given the scraper a good filing, you should have a neat square edge.

Place the scraper flat on the bench, so the squared edge overhangs, then use a burnisher to rub down the flat sides by drawing it across the top of the scraper with even pressure. With the scraper still held over the edge of the bench, and the burnisher at a 45-degree angle to the edge, draw the burnisher with even pressure across the edge of the scraper. This has the effect of turning over the nice sharp burr we want. Some use the back of a gouge, but we recommend using a burnisher because it avoids potential injury.

All four edges of the flat scraper can be sharpened in this way. Curved or shaped scrapers are also very useful and are sharpened in the same way.

1 Begin by flattening the back. If the chisel does not have a flat back, you are going to find it difficult to get a good edge. You do not need to flatten the whole back of the chisel – this would take a long time. You are only interested in an inch or so near the edge.

2 Place a centimetre of the blade on to the stone, pushing down firmly with the first two fingers of the left hand (if you are right-handed) so that the back rests flat on the stone. The right hand is the motor that drives the sharpening process; the left hand keeps the contact. You must be careful not to accidently lift the chisel; if you do this, you will simply be creating sharpening work... long, tedious sharpening work...

3 Movement on to the stone as you sharpen should undulate between 1–2cm, which will prevent getting a ridge on the back. If you were to make a jig to hold the chisel at 1cm, you would end up with a little step on the back of the chisel – not good. How will you know if the back of the chisel is flat? One way is to take a permanent marker and colour the back of the chisel. As you sharpen, you will see low points with ink still in them.

4 Flip the chisel over and press the bevel to the stone, using two fingers as before. Move the chisel in a figure of eight across the stone, taking care to keep finger pressure so that the chisel remains in contact. Eventually a burr will form, where the edges meet. If you do not have a burr, it means that the edges are not meeting and you will not get a sharp edge. If this happens you will need to go back to flattening again.

5 Once you have a nice edge you can go to jeweller's rouge and a leather strop, which finishes off the process by removing any remaining burr.

Materials

Wood

When a violin is made, the back and front are often made from two pieces of wood. The wood is cut from the tree in what is called a quarter cut. A quarter cut is like a wedge of cake, and the violin maker glues the two thick ends of the cake together. This configuration is strong and optimal for production of good tone, and, as an extra bonus, the figure and grain symmetries are also aesthetically pleasing. Some instruments are made from one piece of wood, cut on the slab, like a section through the tree.

Replacement wood

When buying replacement wood, always try to buy the best you can, and it is worth looking around for it on the internet.

Always try to find the appropriate type of wood – spruce for spruce replacement, maple for maple – and choose wood with similar distance on the growth rings so that it will blend well. Also pay attention to how the wood has been cut, as this will affect the way the instrument reflects light. You want the wood that you are putting on to behave in the same way as the surrounding wood, otherwise it will stand out as you move the violin around, especially on the lighter varnishes where the reflectivity of the wood comes through. Finally try to select wood of contemporary age if at all possible.

For a fingerboard, nut or saddle, you are looking for ebony that has been seasoned for as long as possible. See if you can acquire an old cello fingerboard that can be cut down and

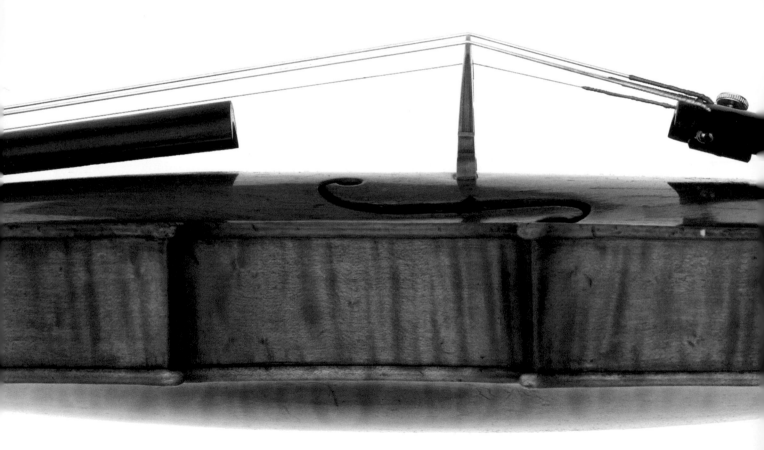

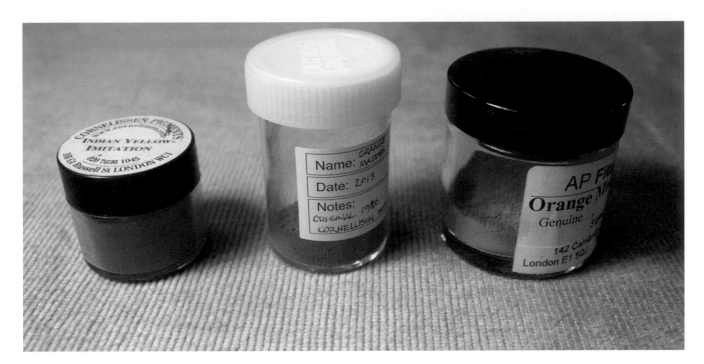

used for a violin – this would certainly be well seasoned as it may have been on the instrument for a hundred years. You are looking for a fingerboard without flame or distinct grain, and preferably as dark as possible. If a fingerboard is highly figured, planing may cause the wood to rip and tear, so make sure you use a low-angle plane with a very sharp blade. In extreme cases a toothed blade may be used initially.

Japanese paper

Japanese paper is used in Japan for screens within a house and is also a very useful and strong material for repairing cracks in a violin. Available in different thicknesses, it is strong because it has long fibres, so it meshes together extremely well. It is similar to glassfibre in this respect, and, like glassfibre, it has a weaker direction. You can find out the weaker direction by ripping the paper, without twisting it, with your fingers – you will find one way is stronger than the other.

When repairing a crack, avoid using the Japanese paper too thickly across the crack, and do not use paper in widths of more than about 10mm because it will distort the crack as it dries. For cracks that will not pull together well, use wooden studs instead.

Colours and pigments

When mixing retouch varnish, you will need to source some good-quality colours. Dried pigments (powdered colours) are getting harder to find, but you can still buy them from good art shops or online.

These are the most useful dried pigments and colours to have:

ABOVE Madder.

- Orange Madder
- Indian Yellow
- Burnt Umber
- Burnt Sienna
- Lamp Black
- Prussian Blue
- Crimson Red
- Titanium White

Watercolours are useful where grain lines need to be retouched and can also be used to paint blemishes on to new wood that has been added.

BELOW Preparing to make pigment.

CHAPTER 4

Buying a violin

In this chapter we will look at the different kinds of instruments on the market and how to identify and assess them.

What is out there?

The first thing to note is that there are a lot of violins from modern factories on the second-hand market. You will commonly see names like Stentor, Stagg, Yamaha and Primavera, and at the more expensive end of the scale another name is Archer.

All these are instruments of reasonable quality in their own right, but they are mass-produced and intended for the student market. You will find examples of these on eBay, in music shops, in antique shops and at car boot sales.

Among older instruments, trade violins are the most common type on the market. During the industrialisation era of the late 19th and early 20th centuries, the demand for violins outstripped the speed at which artisan makers could produce them, so inevitably businesses sprang up that were geared to manufacture instruments quickly and cheaply.

There were two models of mass manufacture. In one model instruments were made in a small factory with work divided up between the workers for efficiency. One worker might make the neck and the scroll, another might prepare and work the ribs, another might work the back, another the front – all the pieces were created separately and then assembled. France predominated in this model, principally at Mirecourt in the Vosges where hundreds of workers were employed in violin-making factories. In the other model, which predominated in Germany and was centred on Mittenwald in Upper Bavaria, instruments were cheaply manufactured in a cottage industry, often using cheap labour from Czechoslovakia, and then sold through a factory dealer.

Buying a violin, new or old, is not necessarily straightforward. You can buy a mass-produced instrument or something more individual, but, whatever you buy, each violin has its own soul and idiosyncrasies.

Some violins may respond to a player in an almost mystical way, and refuse advances from other suitors. This is not to say there is anything supernatural about violins, simply that violins are individual in the same way that humans are individuals. A violin is built within tolerances and to quality levels, each has their own behaviour, and each responds in different ways according to its build and its player.

Also ask yourself which category you fall into – collector, player, restorer or dealer? This will influence what you look for in a violin.

If you are a player, maybe you are interested in particular music styles that may influence both the style of the violin you look at and how it is set up – baroque, orchestral or solo styles

have different requirements. Many luthiers today offer a baroque set-up and there are replica violins with very good sound quality.

A single violin will not be sufficiently adaptable to be used in both orchestral and small chamber playing. For example, when playing an orchestral solo you need a powerful voice so that you can be heard above all the other instruments, but this would be overkill for a chamber quartet. You need to make a decision – or buy more than one violin!

Suppliers and cost

Talk to friends and colleagues, or to your teacher if you are taking lessons, in order to locate a good dealer or maker that will meet your needs. You could also attend a 'maker day' where makers gather to show their skills. The British Violin Making Association (BVMA) runs one in London every year.

Let us consider price. Unfortunately for the player, violins are collectible antiques in their own right, so some old and desirable instruments fetch considerably large and disproportionate price tags. Sound may be the last thing that the collector is concerned with – more important to them is when, where and by whom the violin was made. So if you are a player, we urge you to consider a violin on its own merits, the most important of which, we suggest, should be sound quality and condition.

There are plenty of modern makers producing well-priced instruments that are made with as much care and precision as the old masters, and have very good sound quality as a result. Furthermore, modern makers are able to 'antique' instruments, if you want a violin that appears to have some age. Modern makers do price their instruments realistically: the cost of materials alone may be hundreds of pounds and to create a completed violin requires many hours of intensive precision labour.

Size

We should consider size, and why it is important. Violins do come in different sizes to suit different-sized players. Many players start when they are very young, and will begin with a violin to fit their reach. If the player cannot comfortably reach

OPPOSITE The right violin. *Gresei*

the end of the fingerboard, their ability will suffer and their learning experience will be a tale of misery.

Sizes range from tiny 1/16th violins up to full-size '4/4'. The 1/16th size is for very small children (and satirists), and as children very quickly grow out of this size these baby instruments are rare.

Appearance

Appearance may be the thing that draws you to an instrument in the first instance and it is good to look for something that you feel inspires you. But we must emphasise that if you are serious about spending your hard-earned cash on an instrument, always go and look at it, play it and borrow it or rent it if at all possible. Do not buy an instrument on the basis of a photograph because you cannot really know if you and the instrument are suited unless you at least take it out to lunch first, metaphorically speaking.

As well as the varnish and the finish, look at the quality of the corners and how well the f-holes are cut.

Tactile impressions

When you pick up the instrument, feel its weight. Consider the neck weight and balance as you position it to play. Does the neck feel smooth? Can you run your thumb unimpeded along the neck? Do your fingers fall comfortably on to the fingerboard? How thick does the neck feel?

Audio quality

Your own ears are the best judge of a violin's audio quality. If your ears refuse to play ball, take along someone who can discern the tonal differences. If the arch is high the tone is sweet; if the arch is low there will be more power. If you try an instrument and you feel the tone is great but it is lacking in power, communicate your needs to the maker or seller – they may be able to do something about it.

BELOW The buyer's toolkit.

Upgrading

It is tempting to buy other new things with your new violin purchase, but this can be a mistake. Do not be cajoled into buying a new bow at the same time as buying a new violin. Sticking with your old bow will allow you to feel the difference with your new instrument and you will get more out of the experience of playing. Furthermore it will save you the price of a new bow.

We give the same advice for a case. If your old case is perfectly serviceable, it does not need to be replaced. Enjoy your new violin purchase as it is, and in time you can upgrade other things.

Buyer's toolkit

A small toolkit that you can carry with you in a pocket will help you decide if an instrument is right for you, and here are our suggested items:

- **Jeweller's loupe or magnifying glass** A loupe is very useful for close inspection of an instrument. For example, you will be able to look for areas where the violin may have been repaired, and you will be able to inspect the quality of the purfling.
- **Pen torch** By shining it at different angles on to cracks and blemishes, you will quickly be able to see if there is more or less than meets the eye.
- **Cloth tape measure** A handy little cloth tape measure will be useful for checking the dimensions of the violin. Is the neck too short? Is the bridge in the right place? Is the violin wider than you imagined?
- **Pen and paper** It is useful to scribble down your impressions of an instrument on the day you look at it. If you decide to put off the purchase for another day, you can revisit your thoughts, and you are also less likely to forget things if you make notes immediately after the visit.

A second opinion is always helpful so take a violin-playing friend or relative with you when looking at instruments. When you find a violin that appeals, have your companion listen to you play, have them play and you listen, and garner their opinion. The second opinion will help you be objective in what can be an emotion-driven purchase. A musical friend with a good ear will also be able to help determine what best suits your playing style and needs. Is there plenty of power and is the tone bright, sweet and resonant, or as musical as a frog singing in custard? It is preferable to try out the violin with your own bow (and rosin) rather than one proffered by the vendor, as this will give you a better idea of how it is going to feel when you get it home.

If you are considering trade-in, sometimes dealers and makers will offset the cost of the new instrument. If your violin is in good shape, they will be able to resell it and your old instrument will continue its own journey from player to player.

Where to buy

There are numerous places to buy a violin, and it really depends on what you want to do with the instrument and how much risk you are willing to take. If you go to antique shops you will often see violins there, but on most occasions you will find that they are not of high quality or they are modern violins, and sometimes you will see ludicrous price tags on things that are just not worth a second look.

Auctions

Good auction houses offer a wide range of older violins, but you must know what you are looking at and what to look for. You will also be in competition with collectors and dealers, and prices can sometimes be driven up.

Knowledge is the key. There are good instruments to be had at reasonable prices if you know what to look for. Do your homework and have a look through *The Red Book*, a detailed guide to prices achieved at auctions in Europe and the USA. Many auction houses provide photographs and descriptions of their instruments online, so you can take your time and do some research at home before you go to the viewing.

Go to the viewing well in advance of the auction, and look at the instruments that interest you. You will find that most auction houses will have an open viewing that allows you to handle and play the instruments. But avoid showing your

BELOW AND RIGHT Violins displayed for inspection prior to an auction.

enthusiasm if you think you have found something worth bidding on – you may tip off a competitor! If you do intend to bid, take a note of the lot numbers and be aware that auction houses often charge a buyer's premium, which is a percentage on the sale price of the instrument. Also check if there are any other costs, such as VAT.

Study the payment and possession terms. One enterprising but inexperienced auction-goer ended up buying five antique violins and it transpired that he needed to collect them on the day of purchase, which would have been fine had he not decided to cycle to the auction house that day. If you cannot meet the possession terms, the auction house may accommodate you – for a price. You will have to pay storage and administration charges that will accumulate the longer you delay. So be organised!

Finally there is some auction terminology that you should understand:

- **'Attributed to'** This means that the valuer thinks the instrument shows the quality and characteristics of a particular maker's work. 'Attributed to Gagliano', therefore, means that in an expert's opinion Gagliano made the violin because it displays his characteristics.
- **'The workshop of'** This means that the valuer does not know who it was made by, but does know that it was produced at the workshop of a particular maker or factory.
- **'The school of'** This is more general and means that the violin has particular traits of a region, but cannot be placed to any particular maker.

Online

Buying online, through an auction site such as eBay or from a trader, is great if you are happy to take a risk or want to buy a neglected instrument on which to practise repair and restoration. The problems with online buying, though, are obvious: it is difficult to try out the instrument, your only recourse if you buy an unsuitable instrument on eBay is likely to be resale, and you take a risk because you never know exactly what you are going to get until it is delivered. And then there is the delivery lottery; although only a small number of parcels get damaged or go missing, ensure you have insurance.

Reputable dealers

A reputable dealer will carry a selection of instruments and will offer you a good service, but they will probably not be able to offer any tailoring and may refer you to a maker or restorer if you need something special. That said, violin makers often sell their instruments through dealers.

Reputable makers

A maker will be able to tailor an instrument to your needs, and help you with your choice. They will often have a selection of instruments to try, and provide a more personal service. If you want to find a good maker, start by looking at the BVMA website and attend the annual 'maker day'. Some makers specialise in particular styles of violin, others may concentrate on a particular master pattern such as the old Cremonese style.

Reputable restorers

A good restorer is the safer source when purchasing an older instrument. A restorer is likely to be intimate with the violin, may have done repair work on it, may also know where it has been repaired in the past, and will have information about its provenance where this is known.

Private purchase

Inevitably you will come across an advert in the paper for a violin, and, armed with the knowledge and guidance in this book, you can feel confident about responding to it. To save a wasted journey, ask the seller questions over the phone to determine what kind of violin they think they have and its likely condition. Here is a checklist:

- Does it have a label? This will tell you what it is not…
- Does it have a case that came with it? This will tell you if it has been carefully stored.
- How long has it been in their possession?
- Where was it bought? Auction, local music store, friend of a friend?
- Does it have any damage or problems they know of?
- How much did it cost when it was bought? They might not divulge this, but it is worth asking.
- How often has it been played? This will give a clue to how well it might work and how much action it has seen.
- Where is it stored? Garage, shed, attic, under the bed?
- Does it come with a bow? Newer student violins are often supplied with a bow.
- Is it a full-size violin? If they do not know, ask them to measure it for you.

Completing a transaction

If you are buying an older instrument, ask the seller if it comes with a valuation for insurance purposes. This will normally be provided on the dealer's headed paper. You may also ask for evidence of provenance and any known history of damage repair.

New instruments will probably be supplied with a warranty; the maker wants to make sure you are happy. You should check what the warranty actually covers.

Common problems

When buying a violin, you need to look closely at the instrument for signs of damage or repair. Minor scratches and scuffs can be remedied satisfactorily, as can small dents. These are more or less aesthetic problems that are not structural and should not be great impediments to your purchase decision, so treat them positively as negotiation points with the seller.

There are, however, quite a few severe problems that may not be apparent to the casual observer. These are structural, can cost a lot to put right, and are described in the sections that follow.

ABOVE Edge damage.

BELOW Varnish crackling.

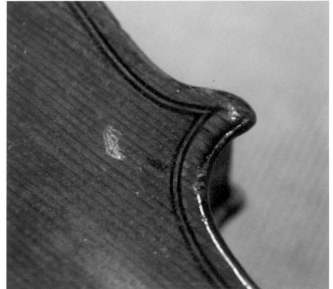

ABOVE A minor dent.

BELOW An f-hole crack.

Collapsed front arching

Collapsed front arching is caused by the continual pressure of the bridge and strings on the front of the violin. Over time this can deform the front and collapse the arch. You will be able to spot this by looking where the bridge stands – the natural arch will appear flattened where the wood has failed.

Sound post crack

A sound post crack is caused by the pressure of the sound post on the front of the violin. This weakens the front and affects tone and power. If left untreated, it may eventually result in complete failure of the front, which is expensive to repair as the front needs to be removed and the crack area cleaned, repaired and patched to reinforce the wood. The same can happen to the back of the instrument; this type of damage is usually caused by an impact in the sound post area.

Cracked peg box

A peg-box crack is often caused by ill-fitting pegs and unnecessary pressure, and in extreme cases requires a complete graft. Most, however, can be repaired using techniques to reinforce the peg box and spiral bushing.

TOP LEFT A nasty crack indeed.

LEFT Repairing a sound post crack.

BELOW LEFT Putting in a sound post patch.

BELOW A finished sound post patch.

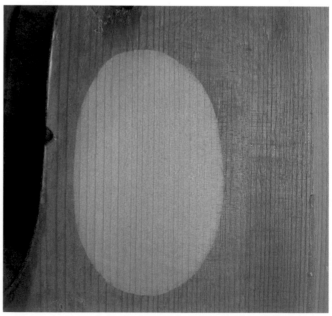

ABOVE A bushed peg box.

ABOVE Detail of bushing.

Any repair needs to be strong enough to withstand the wear and tear of peg tuning and unfortunately this requires replacement of a lot of the original wood, although some modern restorers are developing new techniques that have the required strength and preserve more of the original wood.

Button crack

A button crack is another expensive problem to avoid. A crack of this nature must be repaired with a button patch, a process that involves removal of the back of the violin. This is major surgery, and expensive; in fact some restorers may be unwilling to undertake such work. If you do decide to go ahead with purchase, find out the cost of repair and negotiate with the seller.

Woodworm

You should avoid instruments with woodworm damage as the wood will have been severely weakened and there may be more damage that is not visible. Woodworm, which is formed by the larva of a beetle that feeds on wood, is characterised by tiny exit holes of 1.5–2mm in diameter where the larva has made its escape.

You may also see woodworm tracks on thin areas of wood such as violin ribs. This can be bad news, as a violin rib is only around 1–1.5mm thick to begin with.

Laminated fronts

Some cheap violins are made of laminate rather than solid wood, because it can be pressed into the arch shape required rather than carved out. Take a look in the f-hole and observe the edge of the wood where the f-hole is cut out – here you would be able to see the lamination layers.

There are two problems with this technique. Firstly, it puts stresses into the wood in areas where they do not occur on carved fronts. Secondly, lamination is made up of layers of wood that have been glued together, and will not have quite the same tonal purity as solid wood.

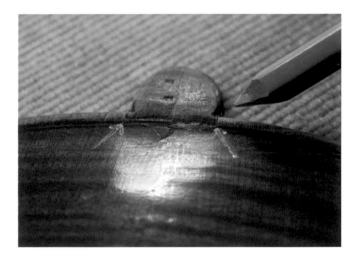

ABOVE A button crack.

BELOW Evidence of woodworm.

Violin identification

As with any quality instrument, you can spend whatever you like on a violin, but the buyer should be aware that the violin has been a victim of fakery, forgery and mistakery.

The authors acknowledge that the word 'mistakery' may not exist in the English language at the time of writing, but contend that it should: violin identification throughout its history has sometimes turned out – truly and innocently – to be plain wrong.

The reasons why violin identification is difficult are numerous but in essence there are three, as follows:

- **Variations in a maker's style and approach** Although there are traits that can be identified, these must be related to the period in which the maker was working and take account of the way the maker's style and approach may have changed as the years passed. Stradivari evolved his style throughout his career and was still experimenting when he expired.
- **Honest copying** Violin makers like to copy existing violin designs. Anyone who studies at a modern violin-making school, for example, is likely to be required to attempt to reproduce an existing master violin design. In fact some makers like to build a new violin based on an existing design, and then go to considerable lengths to make it look old and worn. The intention is not to pull the wool over the eyes of buyers, but simply to create something that is beautiful and in keeping with the concept of the violin.
- **Fakery and forgery** Because of the value of violins, forgery and fakery is rife, and some of the work is very, very good, enough to fool all but the most meticulous of experts.

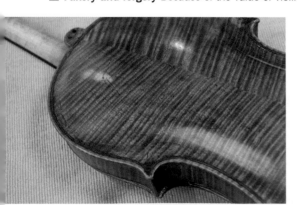

LEFT A pleasing flame.

Labels

If you look inside a violin through the f-hole on the bass side you will often find a label bearing information about where, when and by whom the violin was made. More often than not, this information can only be used as final confirmation of origin that has been already determined through evidence and observation.

Why do we make this point? Well, throughout Europe there were many violin makers emulating Stradivari, and labelling their violins with such gems as:

Antonious Stradivarius Cremonensis
Faciebat anno 1713
Made in Czechoslovakia

We assert that Stradivari never visited Czechoslovakia in the 18th century, our principal reasons for this view being, firstly, that the Czech region was not a popular holiday resort at the time and, secondly and compellingly, Czechoslovakia did not actually exist until 1918.

This particular label was created for an instrument based on a style of the great maker Stradivari, but is honest enough to state where the violin was made. Other copiers in history have not been so honest, due to the great value placed on certain makers' instruments. Some luthiers have strayed into the grey area, by restoring and changing existing instruments to pass them off as something they are not.

On the label, note a couple of mistakes. 'Stradivarius' is the Latinised version of Stradivari; Stradivari himself used 'Stradiuarius', with a 'u' in the middle. And 'Cremonensis' would have been written as 'Cremonenfis', with the first 's' rendered like a modern 'f'.

Thus armed, we know that we cannot really trust labels, even those that are completely correct, except to help us show that an instrument is not what it purports to be.

Authenticity

If buying an expensive instrument with a history, it may come with a certificate of authenticity. You should check the origin of the certificate, exactly who has put their name to it, and verify that they actually did. If you can establish that a trustworthy expert has authenticated the instrument, then all well and good.

One difficulty occurs if the creator of the authentication documents is dead, as you will then be relying on the provenance of those certificates. Another difficulty is marrying a genuine certificate of authenticity with the instrument that it describes. Finally we should point out that appraisals and certification are opinions of experts, and sometimes even the experts are not 100 per cent correct because there have been so many violin makers emulating, borrowing and copying from each other.

Recognition characteristics

The guidance that follows briefly outlines some of the traits of the particular schools of violin making. If you wish to learn more, there are many good reference books and online resources that delve more deeply into this fascinating area.

Violin manufacture

There are, broadly speaking, three categories of violin manufacture that apply both to modern violins and to violins produced centuries ago:

- **Artisan violins** Created by professional makers and workshops, artisan violins range in quality depending on the skill, patience and sobriety of the maker. Modern luthiers typically produce a handful of instruments a year, sometimes commissioned, sometimes experimenting. They may have studied formally at a school of violin making, via apprenticeship, as well as from books and literature.
- **Factory-produced violins** Factory production of violins began in the 19th century during the industrial revolutions and were produced to meet growing demand. They had to be produced efficiently and sometimes to a price, so corners were cut and generally the level of quality was not as high as artisan-produced violins. Modern factory-produced violins are built as standard for students and are excellent starter instruments on which many musicians have begun their careers. You can walk into almost any music shop and buy one, and it will be set up to an acceptable standard and playable 'out of the box'.
- **Amateur-made violins** Finally there are the amateur makers who may begin informally and reach a sufficiently good standard to produce playable violins. Some go on to study professionally, and become very good violin makers. Others produce a few instruments when time allows.

Most 'trade' violins were made in France and Germany. You can normally tell French trade violins from German ones because the craftsmanship is better.

The French trade was more standardised and the measurements of French violins are normally more precise. For example, the neck length from the end of the plate to the end of the fingerboard is supposed to be 130mm on a full-size instrument and you would expect a French violin to be within

1mm of this, while the back length will be around 355mm and the f-stop will be around 195mm. So your first step in recognising a violin's origins is to take measurements and compare them with the ideal size. Measurements on a German trade violin will be erratic: for example, the neck length may be as much as 10mm out, and f-holes may be sporadically placed on the instrument without any real care.

The reason behind all this is that the French were working in much more controlled conditions and a workshop manager would ensure that the employees kept their work within the acceptable tolerances. In Germany, violin making was more of a cottage industry, and the quality varied depending on who was making the instrument or its parts. There were also imported instruments from Czechoslovakia cheaply assembled and sold through the workshops in Germany.

In the early part of the 20th century a lot of manufactured instruments came out of Czechoslovakia and Romania, and the quality really did suffer. Instruments were sometimes just pressed out instead of carved. The manufacturers steam-pressed the back and front to deform the wood, and as a result the centre join tends to fail as it is under too much pressure from the deformation process.

BELOW Violin by Francois Medard, a French 17th century maker. *Chi Mei Museum*

French trade making

The workmanship of a French trade violin differs from that of a German instrument in many ways.

French violins have very distinct edgework; by this we mean the outline of the instrument – how the curves flow and how the edges are finished. The French produce fairly crisp edgework, in keeping with a reasonable level of quality. The varnish you will find is fairly flat and dull. French instrument varnish tends to have a lot of colour that is quite intense and an orangey brown. The choice of wood is normally good; the French liked to see nicely figured wood on both the back and the ribs.

French makers tended to use planes with toothed blades, which left characteristic tooth marks on underside surfaces, like a combed effect. Toothed plane blades have the advantage over straight blades in that they tend not to rip up the wood and are very good for fine work. If you have a cello and suspect it to be French, try feeling under the fingerboard and you might detect the little grooves made by a toothed plane. This work was often

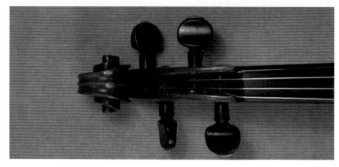

ABOVE French making, scroll work.

done at Mirecourt, the town in the Vosges that is known for the manufacture of musical instruments.

Sometimes the French may blacken the inside of the f-hole and also the rib corners. The chamfer on the scroll may also be blackened to emphasise the scroll – Stradivari did the same thing.

ABOVE French making, a nicely flamed back.

ABOVE French making, attention to detail and line.

German trade making

German instruments used more varied wood – sometimes very plain, sometimes highly flamed – depending on whatever was available at the time.

German makers tended to try to age the instrument to improve its appearance. However, the faking was very predictable and was repeated from instrument to instrument. Around the C-bouts on the back and front, for example, there will be uniform black marks to give the impression of ingrained dirt. With real dirt you get different levels of shade; with German fake dirt, you get one shade of black all over the instrument.

Another 'antiquing' technique is to introduce artificial wear patterns on the wood. With genuine wear, a player's hand, shoulders and neck rub away the varnish over time through repetitive use, and on an older instrument the varnish may have worn through to bare wood, although someone may have put a clear coat of varnish over the bare wood. With German faked wear, you will see the standard patterns of wear but these will have been varnished over.

On old instruments the corners can wear over time. The varnish wears away first, and then the actual wood wears away.

German makers tried to imitate this wear artificially, by cutting in the corners and then varnishing over the wear work. But, as we have said, on a genuinely old instrument the first thing that comes off is the varnish! So you should never find a worn corner that has retained varnish, unless it has been revarnished – which you can tell. Compared with French violins, German varnish tends to be more muddy brown in colour.

As discussed in an earlier section, many German instruments have fictitious labels announcing that they are Stradivari, Stainer, Bergonzi, Amati or whatever; the common ones are Stradivari and Stainer. Stainer-type violins are sometimes crudely stamped under the button on the back. Another common copy is Maggini, recognised by double purfling and an extra turn on the scroll. But if you were to compare the copies to the real instruments, you would see major differences.

German edgework is fairly rough and certainly less precise and crisp than that of the French. The shape of the button at the back of the instrument can resemble a gothic revival door, or a church door, with a pinched arch instead of the nice rounded shape found on French instruments. The button can be tiny and sometimes slopes away from the instrument when viewed from the side. The heel of the neck can also be heavily scalloped.

Another characteristic is the scrollwork. Underneath the chin of the scroll the volute stops long before it gets too far into the throat. The reason is that the further you get into the throat, the more difficult it is to get a good crisp finish – it is easier and quicker just to stop.

Sometimes you will find that the bass bar is stuck in without any real thought. Alternatively you may find that the bass bar is integrated – carved out of the front of the violin. An integrated bass bar is not as strong because the grain runs in the direction of the front, being the same piece of wood, and thus there is not the reinforcement that a fitted bass bar provides. As a result integral bass bars have to be left much thicker for the same strength, and thus weight is added to the instrument. A fitted bass bar can be made more slender as it is fitted across the grain of the front, and there is a lot of strength in this without thickness.

Occasionally you will find German instruments without any corner blocks inside, and there may also be no linings to reinforce the ribs. Every so often a German maker only put in bottom blocks, omitting the blocks at the top and sides. Occasionally, just for show, they would even fit fake blocks that were not attached to the ribs at all; on such a violin you may see a hollow between the ribs and the block if you were to remove the front. One can only conclude that the tonal quality of these instruments suffered from such crude manufacturing techniques.

Notwithstanding the foregoing, we should emphasise at this point that there are no golden rules, and that there are always

ABOVE Some artificial antiquing on this German trade back.

ABOVE A heavily scalloped heel

ABOVE The 'gothic revival door shape'

exceptions to everything we have outlined. What you should always do when trying to identify an unknown instrument is to cross-reference other instruments. For instance, consider an instrument with these features:

■ Non-standard measurements all over the place.
■ The carving work does not go very far under the scroll.
■ The f-holes do not have any fluting on the wings.
■ There is obvious fake antiquing in black.
■ The joint for the ribs is in the middle.
■ The corners are rounded over.

This will probably be a German trade violin. But be careful, because actually you may be holding something quite early, and quite valuable. You can find really old instruments with measurements that are all over the place.

English making

The English did not have a factory production model. Instead they had much better skilled workshops where good craftsmen were employed. Instruments were individually hand-made without the production-line mentality, so the quality was generally better. For example, in the late 18th century John Betts employed quite a few notable makers – Richard Tobin (of Irish descent) was one – and he also acquired some good early instruments for his workforce to copy.

A characteristic of English-made instruments is their varnish, which can look very muddy and opaque. Early English work, however, can look quite interesting and the varnish on early English viols is often very pleasing, rivalling some of the best Italian varnish of the period. English makers tended not to bother with purfling. The best-quality instruments would be inlaid, while others might just feature purfling on the front but not the back, or they might have painted-on purfling.

The English preferred to use boxwood in the centre of the purfling instead of the more traditional pear wood. Boxwood has a nice warm, deep orange-yellow colour and is a very pleasing wood to behold. Interestingly, old chisel handles can be found in boxwood and these have a really lovely patina developed through continued handling and age. This same pleasing patina develops in boxwood purfling and it stands out in a most striking way.

English instruments tend to be wider across the C-bout. If you think you have an English viola or cello made by someone like Kennedy, you may observe that the instrument appears particularly wide across the C-bout. This looks really pleasing for English violas, because what is lacked in length is compensated for in width, and they have a lovely warm sound as a consequence.

Early English instruments can be a little pinched on the arching, so they lend themselves more to chamber music because the volume is just not there, but the tone is sweet. Generally a higher arch gives the sweeter sound, whereas a lower arch projects more volume from the instrument. Stradivari lowered the arch on his later designs to improve the sound projection, creating an instrument that was more powerful and suited to solo performance.

You may find English sycamore instead of maple used for the back of the instrument. They are related tree species and it is quite hard to tell the difference between the two.

If you have an instrument with the front or back removed, or are able to peer into an instrument via the end-pin hole, you will see that the blocks on the inside are quite characteristic in their half-round shape – imagine a section of pole cut in two down the middle with one half used for the top block and the other half for the bottom. You may also find on occasion that the corner blocks are relatively tiny compared with those used by other makers.

Another characteristic is at the peg box, where the shape may flare out as it drops to the back wall of the peg box instead of being perfectly straight and parallel. It is this kind of subtlety in aesthetics that you can look for in any instrument, and can be appreciated by the trained eye. But a word of warning: watch out for modern fakes as the rogues are getting more and more clever at copying all of these traits.

From time to time English makers used antiquing to make an instrument look as though it had aged, and the results of their efforts are in complete contrast to the German 'knock-off' approach to antiquing.

LEFT A violin by English maker Jacob Rayman, circa 1645. *Chi Mei Museum*

Italian making

The Italian makers were established in the main regions of Brescia, Cremona, Milan, Naples and Venice. In Cremona there were also three categories of maker, defined as Old Cremonese (makers contemporary to Stradivari, Guarneri, etc), Modern Cremonese (from the late 19th century to the 1930s) and 'Modern-Modern' Italian (1930s onwards).

First of all we will cover some generalisations about Cremonese making. The bottom rib of a Cremonese violin will be one piece and so will the top rib. It is quite easy to see this on the bottom rib: no join will be visible either side of the end pin. On other violins you will see a join where the two pieces of rib meet. The only variation to this on a Cremonese violin occurs where the instrument has shrunk, in which case the bottom rib is carefully taken off the bottom block, cut, a section removed, and then the rib is re-glued with a join at the bottom block. As the neck interrupts the top rib, it is difficult to determine whether or not it was a single piece at the time of construction.

One of the main identifiers of Cremonese work is the varnish. Italian varnish is probably the best-looking violin varnish. There is something about the ground and varnish that is absolutely fantastic to behold. Italian makers used an oil-based varnish originally and at some point swapped to a spirit varnish, probably because of the prolonged drying time required for oil varnishes. With spirit varnish, the spirit evaporates quickly, almost as it is applied, leaving the colour in place. Some surviving letters written by Stradivari indicate a long waiting time for delivery of an instrument because of the drying time of the varnish – but this may have been an excuse because he was behind on his work!

The choice of wood on an old Cremonese violin is interesting. Usually the grain on the back is very faint compared with a cheap instrument, where the grain is quite strong and readily apparent. On a good-quality Cremonese instrument you still get the flame but not the grain, indicating that the wood these makers were using was very slow-growing, which made it very fine-grained and thus of high quality.

Gagliano of the Neapolitan school used black paper in the purfling instead of dyed pear wood. Some instruments also feature a two-piece back that was jointed on the slab instead of being made from quarter-sawn wood – most unusual and interesting-looking.

Work from the Modern Cremonese era has a bit more flair to it. For instance, if you look at the scrolls on a violin from the Ventepane school, the carving comes all the way down to the peg box rather than stopping on the turns of the scroll. You

ABOVE Scroll detail of the 1709 Viotti Marie by Strad. *Chi Mei Museum.*

might also find f-holes with a slight lean, or with more style on the wings, or with the scroll coming further down on the fluting.

The Modern Cremonese instruments have certainly left their own mark, but in some cases the footprint is too heavy, with an excess of modification that destroys the clean aesthetics of the violin. In our opinion it is good to leave individuality in violin making, but it should be done in a way that can be appreciated aesthetically and without being immediately apparent when the violin is played. If a maker deviates too far from the traditional violin shape, then they are possibly creating unplayable instruments, or ones that are offensive to the eye.

Developing your eye

It normally takes some years of practice and training to develop an eye for the different schools of instruments. The best training is through study. You can practise by looking at a lot of instruments – and pictures of instruments – and by handling a lot of instruments. You can talk to makers and dealers for tips on what to look for, and how they distinguish one instrument from the next.

We highly recommend going to instrument auctions, where you can inspect and hold many different instruments, some with known provenance, some without. Handling instruments is a lot more educational than just looking at pictures. Auctioneers who regularly hold instrument sales in the UK include Tarisio, Gardiner Houlgate, Sothebys and Bonhams. These will generally be held in London, but if you live elsewhere you may find that there are local auctions that you can attend.

The bottom line is this: if you wish to recognise instruments you must first teach yourself to observe. Let us describe some outline steps you can take when identifying an unknown instrument.

First of all, determine whether you think it is a trade instrument using the guidelines we presented earlier in this chapter under the heading 'Recognition characteristics' as well as the following pointers:

- **Varnish** Feel its texture and observe its colour and depth of finish, and how the light is reflected.
- **Corners** How well are they defined? Are they crisp? Is there fake wear?
- **The f-holes** Look at how they are cut and their shape, character and position. Do they lean out or in? Are they petite? Are they huge? Are they placed well on the front? Are they symmetrical or is one higher than the other? Does the front near the f-holes have fluting?
- **Scroll** Is it heavy? Is it sharp? How many turns? What is the size of the eye relative to the scroll? Does the carving go deep into the throat?
- **Purfling** Does it flow nicely around the instrument? Is it laid in crudely? Is it drawn on? Are there well-fashioned bee-stings? Which wood has been used?

As you progress, you will find that the first thing you develop is the ability to spot instruments that do not warrant any further investigation. These will be violins made by unskilled amateurs and copyists, and really poor trade instruments. The measurements will be helpful indicators, but your eye will begin to tell you if the neck is 10mm too short, or the f-holes are off-centre and poorly executed.

If a violin under scrutiny does not look like a trade instrument, try to work out its country of origin. You can do this by looking through books and past auction catalogues – printed or online – to find instruments with similar characteristics. Importantly, you should not just look at one instrument from the maker, because the maker will have varied its output and will not have made exactly the same instrument every time. So you need to develop an eye to look at the overall characteristics of a maker. If you think you have an Amati, then you need to look at more than one Amati example because you will never find a carbon copy of what you hold in your hands.

A final observation: there is crudeness in the work on early instruments that is actually very pleasing to behold to the experienced eye. There is a quality to the speed of work done by an experienced hand that does not know any better. The best analogy might be Picasso: he could actually draw well, but his art was made with a very free but experienced hand, and this comes through when you look at his work. The same is true of fine woodworking – you can learn to appreciate skill in all its forms.

Professional opinion

If you are not quite sure about the origins of an instrument that interests you, it can be a good idea to take it to a violin restorer for a valuation. Needless to say, you may get a difference of opinion if you take it to more than one valuer. Besides having a valuation, you will also have expert opinion on the instrument, including some understanding of why they have reached their particular conclusions.

Determining age

The methods for determining the age of an instrument are fraught with problems. Radio-carbon dating, for instance, relies on the destruction of the sample material, and even though modern advances have brought a reduction in the required sample size, it still means taking a chunk out of your violin!

The other difficulty with radio-carbon dating is that it is inaccurate for the dates that we are interested in – around 1700 to present – because changes in the amount of carbon 14 in the environment disrupt the calculation. So radio-carbon technology is pretty hopeless for all but the earliest instruments.

But all is not lost: we still have a few tricks and technologies that we can apply to help us make sense of an instrument. The wood light test and dendrochronology are our two extra tools of choice.

Wood light test

There is a little test you can do with tungsten lights that relies on how the structure of the wood changes with age, and how this affects the transmission of light through the wood.

Take off the end pin, remove the instrument's strings, and look through the end-pin hole. Holding the top bout up to the tungsten light, you are going to be looking at light transmission into the instrument wood. Be careful not to hold it there for too long as you do not want to heat the instrument and potentially blister the varnish. The amount of light that comes through the wood will give an indication of the age of the wood.

In general, the less light that comes through, the older the wood is, regardless of the type of wood. If the whole instrument glows a pinky colour, it will have been made very recently. With an instrument that is 200 or more years old, you are unlikely to see any light coming through at all. The reason behind these differences is that over time the oxidisation process in the wood prevents light from penetrating it. This procedure will only work on a violin because the wood is relatively thin.

Dendrochronology

Dendrochronology is the study of tree rings, specifically the width and spacing of tree rings. Using this information, it is possible to date a piece of wood precisely.

Knowledge that trees have rings that exhibit an annual growth pattern was established in the Renaissance period, although it was probably recognised earlier but not written down.

However, it was not until the 1930s that pioneer researcher A.E. Douglas used a technique called cross dating to establish a long chronology, thereby marking the beginnings of dendrochronology. This was followed up by the work of M.G.L. Baillie and J.R. Pilcher, who were able to take us back some 10,000 years by using Irish bog oak as their source of ancient trees. Bog oak occurs where trees are preserved from decay in peat bogs due to the anaerobic conditions and high acidity of the peat.

A cross section through a tree trunk will reveal rings of annual growth. In some years a tree will grow quickly and vigorously (wide rings) and in others it will grow slowly (narrow rings). These variations occur in response to a host of climatic and environmental influences. If a significant number of trees is sampled in an area, these growth patterns can be averaged into a chronology for that area, showing the general trend of growth over the years.

For a recently felled tree, you can work backwards from the present day (the outermost ring) deep into the past (the very first ring near the centre of the tree), with each ring generally corresponding to a year of growth. For very old trees you can go back a long way in time: the bristle-cone pine found in the USA is the oldest living tree known and some specimens have been alive for some 4,500 years.

But we can go beyond this. Trees that have fallen because of old age or other influences lie upon the ground holding their own secrets, perhaps for a very long time. Their lifespan, from the moment they first grew to their demise, is recorded in their rings, but how do we know when exactly these trees lived? How long ago did they die and fall?

The answer to this problem is resolved using a technique called cross-correlation. If you think of a set of tree rings as a barcode, over a long period – say 100 years – they will have a distinct pattern of widths. If we take a tree where the date of its felling is known, we can take a pattern of widths and search for that same pattern in a tree whose date is not known. The size of the sample is important here: if we were to sample only 10 rings we would probably find the same pattern everywhere we looked, but a sample of 100 rings – or, better still, 500 rings – provides a very distinct fingerprint.

We can then take our fallen-tree data and look for a match for this fingerprint. If we find a match, we then can place that tree in time. The pattern may occur in the middle of the trunk of a tree, meaning that earlier rings take us further back in time and offer new patterns to seek. By using this method we can probe deep into history, hopping from pattern to pattern.

Techniques of dendrochronology were applied to stringed instruments as early as 1958, but it was not until the work of Peter Klein in the 1980s that any worthwhile results were obtained. John Topham and Derek McCormick followed up with their studies, published in 1997 in the *Journal of Archaeological Science*, demonstrating that dating instruments using dendrochronology was a viable and useful practice. They went on to show not only that dates could be ascertained, but also that other interesting aspects could be revealed – such as where the wood was sourced and how it was used in making an instrument. Did both sides of a violin come from the same tree? Did different instruments come from the same tree? They were even able to establish tentatively that the English makers they studied used a single source of wood – spruce from a particular Alpine region.

Today there are whole university departments dedicated to dendrochronology in its various applications in archaeology, climate studies, ecology, geomorphology and chemistry. It is a recognised scientific method of learning all sorts of interesting things about the past. As Baillie put it, 'The trees don't lie', but we would humbly amend that by adding, 'But they can be misunderstood'.

DIY dendrochronological studies

ABOVE Tree rings are clearly seen on this violin in the white.

It is possible to have a bit of fun and do your own dendrochronological studies.

Set-up
You first need to lay the violin on its back so that you can easily measure the rings. You will need a microscope of around 10–20X magnification. In order to measure the distances between the rings, a calibrated eyepiece or a linear table with measuring scale will also be helpful.

You need to determine which way the tree grew. Are the oldest rings on the inside or the outside of the violin? Generally, but not always, the centre join was the outside of the tree.

Measurement
Carefully measure the rings and record the consecutive distances from the edge to the centre join. Normally you will have around 80 rings to work with. Varnish and tarnish may obscure measurement, so you need to pick a path across the violin that is clear of blemishes and gives you the best data.

You also need to be careful because some rings are false rings, where there is a stop and restart in a year of growth, and sometimes there is a year in which a tree does not grow at all.

You must also take care to measure consistently. Each ring will have a light region blending into a dark region, and then abruptly stopping where growth stops for the winter before the next ring starts with another light region. This trait immediately tells you which rings are the older ones as the light-to-dark transition is in the direction of outward growth of the tree. To measure a ring width, go from the start of a light area to the end of the adjacent dark area – the abrupt termination at the end of growth.

Analysis
Once you have your ring data, you can put away your violin and do some analysis on a spreadsheet. The first thing to do is index or 'detrend' the data, a method whereby growth trends and long-term trends are removed. Doing this produces ring measurements that are compatible from one tree to another, allowing meaningful comparisons to be carried out.

Herein lies some of the skill of the dendrochronologist – understanding how much or how little trend should be mathematically removed from the data. There are numerous indexing methods available to experiment with, such as polynomial, exponential and high-pass filters.

Correlation
The next step in the process is correlating your data with known data. A good source of known data is the International Tree

For violins we do not have to go back so far in history, but the same techniques we have talked about are applied. The spruce fronts of instruments are used to collect data, the two-piece front of a typical violin having been cut from the same tree in most cases. You can measure from the outside of the violin to the centre on both sides to provide a 'barcode', which often shows a high correlation between the two sides.

Nowadays a scanning electron microscope (SEM) can be used to determine the species of wood used. This technique can even distinguish between closely related trees, such as spruce and pine. Normally a tangential and cross-sectional piece of the wood is taken, but in the case of a violin it is usually not possible to do this without damaging or even destroying the instrument. However, it is possible to use silicone casts – termed 'micro-casting' – from the inside of the instrument where the wood is exposed and unvarnished. The cast can be magnified up to 10,000 times under the SEM to reveal the wood structure, right down to cell walls. Determining the species of wood helps to identify the origin of the wood – which is another clue to when an instrument was made because it is known that wood was sourced from distinct regions.

Dendrochronological techniques have been used on perhaps the most famous and controversial violin in the world. The 'Messiah' was attributed to Stradivari, and there is significant and excellent work by Henri Grissino-Mayer and others at the University of Tennessee to support this. However, other studies have disagreed with the claim, using different chronologies in an attempt to prove that the Messiah was made much later than Stradivari's time. This debate, though, is straying beyond the scope of this book!

Ring Databank (http://www.ncdc.noaa.gov/paleo/treering.html), where you can access hundreds of ring measurements and chronologies that have known dates. Selecting the right data for comparison is another skill. There will be little point in selecting data recorded in Scandinavia for wood that you think might have come from Italy. The more rings that match a pattern, the stronger the correlation result – so you are looking for matches beyond 60 rings at the very least.

One method of determining a match is by use of a mathematical tool called a T test, which puts a score of similarity between two data sets with a particular confidence level. The higher the score, the more alike are the two data sets.

The process is to calculate the T value for the data sets in every position. By this we mean that one data set (the known data) is held static and the other data set (your measurements) is 'tried' at every overlap and the result of the T test at each position is recorded. If the score is high and the overlap sample is sufficiently high, this becomes a match of interest.

There are other mathematical tools available such as Principle Component Analysis, a common technique for finding patterns in high-dimension data.

Visual inspection is the next stage. This is again an acquired skill of the dendrochronologist in which the merits of the match are assessed. The human eye, which is much better at pattern recognition than a simple mathematical test, will be able to see the similarities between the data plots.

If the data passes all these tests, a date can be put on the wood of the violin, although this does not necessarily date the instrument. Difficulties arise where the maker used really old wood. An example is Paul Bailly, the French violin maker who is said to have used wood 200 years before his time.

If you have a piece of wood with little variation in ring width from one ring to the next, then these are termed complacent rings. This kind of growth makes it difficult to cross-correlate, as there is no pattern variation. Perhaps this is an additional problem when trying to match violin wood, as the best violin makers by their nature have always looked for wood with a nice even grain, that is with little variation between one ring and the next.

Software is available to help with the analysis and correlation process. COFECHA and Tellervo are free programs that can be used to cross-date violins in this manner, and there are also paid programs such as WINDENDRO and CDENDRO.

BELOW T-test comparison of two data sets.

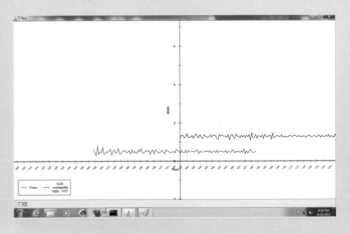

Buying a bow

The first tip we can give about bows is to avoid buying one at the same time as you buy a new violin. You should change things in small increments, a principle that should be followed when changing anything about your violin. This way you will be able to hear the difference that one change can make. If you change many things, you do not know what has made the violin sound better or worse, so the process becomes out of control and unscientific.

When buying a bow, you should first examine the bow from tip to frog; look for any damage and repairs that may have occurred in the bow's life. If you are able to, unscrew the frog and remove it from the bow. Leave the hair in place and check the mortise where the frog lies.

To put the frog back where it belongs, hold the bow by the

ABOVE Damage to the tip of the bow.

BELOW Unscrewing the frog. RIGHT Frog mortise.

end as if you were fishing, and allow the frog to dangle freely from the bow hair. Eventually it will stop spinning with the hair straight, and you can slide it back into its mortise and put the screw back in.

Look down the stick with one eye shut to check that the shape of the stick is straight. Then tighten the bow hair and observe if the bow pulls to the left or the right as you do so. Ideally it should remain central, but if it does have a slight pull, it is better if it pulls to the right-hand side (as you look down the frog to the tip) because that at least aids the playing.

If it is pulling to the left or the right, the hairs may be uneven, causing the tension to be unbalanced, and it is not the bow wood itself that is the problem. This can be corrected by re-hairing the bow so that there are equal numbers of hairs and therefore equal tension.

The key is to ensure that the bow has no damage. It is not impossible to repair bow damage, but it is very difficult and can be costly, depending on the nature of the repair. The frog or the slide can be replaced or repaired if damaged, but the stick and head should be damage-free.

It is best to find a bow with no significant problems to worry about in the first place.

The weight of a violin bow will normally be around 60–62 grams. Each bow also has its own balance point, which will affect how it feels in the hand when you play. Violas and cellos have much heavier, larger bows of around 70 grams for a viola and 80 grams for a cello. It is helpful to feel the difference in these bows so you know what to expect when you are shopping around. The best way to feel the balance of the bow is to play with it   you have the right bow when you do not notice using it.

BELOW Pulling to one side.

BELOW Stick hair slack.

BELOW Stick hair taut.

CHAPTER 5

Basic maintenance

With time and experience, trial and error, you will build up knowledge of your instrument and be able to carry out basic maintenance yourself. All instruments have their own character – some do not like temperature change, some do not like humidity change – so consider your environment before doing anything drastic.

Cleaning

If you own a violin and play regularly, you should try to get into the routine of wiping the violin down with a cloth after each time you play. This will remove sweat and rosin that may harm the finish, and leave your violin in top condition for next time. Keep a good lint-free cloth in the case with the instrument.

ABOVE Cleaning products.   **BELOW** Giving it a good clean.

If during the process of repair it appears that any cleaning of cracks or retouching of varnish is necessary, then cleaning must be done first. This is important because:

Cleaning removes dirt, grease and rosin that may harm the varnish over time. If a violin is left uncleaned, rosin has a habit of sticking to the varnish and can be difficult to remove.

Removal of dirt allows any retouching to match the base colour of the violin, not the colour of the dirt.

If the violin has a fresh crack and is dirty, the crack will inevitably get dirt in it. When cleaning around a crack, avoid rubbing the crack itself as you may push more dirt and rosin into it. Dirt makes a crack harder to glue, and more obvious in a repair job.

Cleaning tools and materials

Here is a list of items you need:

- Metal polish (paste form is best, as creams and fluids tend to end up in cracks – not where you want them).
- Wax/polish remover.
- Cellulose thinners.
- Gloves (chemical-proof ones).
- Cotton buds.
- Soft kitchen towel.
- Vapour mask.
- Carpet or soft cloth.

The cleaning process

Before you start, make sure your work area is clean and well prepared. The environment is important, as you do not want dust and other contaminant sticking to your beautifully cleaned violin.

Place a piece of clean carpet on the bench to protect the violin against knocks and scrapes as you move it around while you clean it.

Wash your hands and put on the protective gloves and face mask. The mask is important because certain chemicals and solvents can give off toxic fumes. You should make sure your work area is well ventilated, as these chemicals can be harmful, and in some cases are also flammable. Ideally you might want to do this outside on a dry, still day.

ABOVE Cleaning tool kit.

In order of increasing potency we have metal polish, wax/polish remover and cellulose thinners. You may not need all these products – it depends on how dirty the violin is.

Test your first chemical in a spot that will not show, either under the chin rest or around the end-pin hole. It is necessary to test chemicals because you do not know how they will react with the varnish, and you may do more harm than good.

Start with the mildest of the cleaning agents, metal polish, which will allow you to remove most light soiling. Put a little on a cotton bud, and rub gently on the violin in the test area to

BELOW Protect yourself and your violin.

ABOVE Metal paste.

see what happens. You should see dirt on your cotton bud after a bit of rubbing. If there is anything other than dirt, this will be varnish colour and you must stop because you are removing the varnish! If all is well, wipe the area with a piece of clean towel.

If metal polish does not remove any dirt, move on to the wax/polish remover. Pour a little into a glass dish, wet your cotton bud, and rub gently on the test area again to check that you are only removing dirt. If dirt still remains, the final stage is the use of cellulose thinners. This is an aggressive cleaning agent so be careful with your test area; wipe the area and again test with

a cotton bud. If you find that either of these cleaning products reacts with the varnish, do not use them – in some cases you may not be able to proceed beyond the metal polish.

Once you have satisfied yourself which cleaning agents will work without damage, you can go ahead and clean the violin. Put a small amount of paste on a piece of kitchen towel and rub the violin, always checking the towel for signs of varnish. Remember to clean around cracks, not over them, as you do not want to introduce dirt and cleaning products into cracks. You need to get right up close to the crack. If you do get the polish in there, it is not the end of the world as the crack will be soaked open and the dirt can be cleaned anyway. Finally, dispose of your soiled kitchen towels outside; cellulose thinners in particular will give off an unpleasant toxic aroma for weeks and is highly flammable.

One final point. Do not over-clean your instrument – it does not need to look like a billiard ball. If the violin is finished with shellac and you polish vigorously, then you are inadvertently French polishing your violin – not what you want to do! This would reduce the authenticity of the finish, and produce an undesirable shine.

If in any doubt about the cleaning process, seek professional advice before inadvertently causing any problems.

ABOVE AND BELOW Cleaning with a cotton bud.

ABOVE AND BELOW Applying thinners with kitchen towel and the effect afterwards.

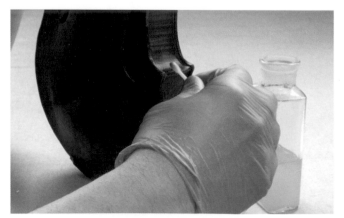

Environment

Instruments are pieces of fine woodwork and, being made of natural materials, are subject to their response to the environment. Wood responds to light, temperature and humidity, and can distort and move with changes in these parameters. As an instrument with particular requirements for set-up and playability, a violin will react and alter of its own accord. In this section we look at each of these behaviours in turn.

Heat variation

Changes in temperature, such as when the instrument is moved from a warm house into the cold on the way to a recital, can cause some problems. Sudden changes of temperature are not good for an instrument. As a general rule of thumb, an instrument will need tuning just before you play it, and it is a good idea to slacken off the strings if you are leaving it unplayed for any period of time.

With some instruments a peg can get stuck with changes in temperature. The worst thing you can do if this happens is to take pliers to the peg. Even if you cover the peg with lots of padding, you will probably still damage it. In the worst-case scenario, the use of too much force can cause a crack in the peg box, which is very costly to repair.

If you leave a violin in a cold house, the low temperature can cause the elevation of the violin neck above the front to change, and in some cases it can move so much that the violin becomes completely unplayable. The neck may have to be reset to correct this problem. You will not see any damage to the instrument with this problem, so it can catch you completely unawares.

Baking

If you leave your instrument in a car on a really hot day, the temperature will increase within the case. This may cause the front and back to unglue from the ribs – not a big problem as this is relatively easy to reglue. The fingerboard can also pop off in the heat, but again this is not a great concern. But either of these problems will leave you with unnecessary expense and the inconvenience of being without your instrument while it is repaired.

If you do have to leave your instrument in a car in hot weather, open the case slightly to let the air flow, and, most importantly, try not to expose it to direct sun. But you should, of course, avoid having to leave your instrument in the car not only for these reasons but also because it is a temptation for theft. To a thief, every violin is a Stradivari and so any violin is worth pinching.

Another problem that can occur with heat, particularly with newer instruments, is that the varnish can become sticky, and this may cause the imprint from the inside of the case to be left on the varnish.

A cautionary tale

There once was a student who left his violin in its case at the workshop during a long vacation. The hapless instrument was left in the sun by the window and happily baked in its case for about a month. Upon returning to the workshop, the unwitting student carefully opened the case to reveal the instrument in all its glory. Carefully grasping the neck he reverently removed the instrument from the case and held it up to the light to admire the beautiful varnish finish he had invested so much effort in. The varnish, however, had remained in the case.

So do not leave your case near a radiator, a fire, in the car or in the window, for your instrument does not like extremes of heat and cold and will repay your carelessness in full.

Light

Violin makers are very conscious of making and using good varnish that does not fade in light, but over time the colour will always fade. You can prevent, or at least delay, the fading process by avoiding exposure of your violin to the sun for long periods. It is all right for sunlight to touch the violin occasionally as the fading process is a gradual one.

Madder root, which is often used for making violin varnish, is regarded as light-fast and therefore is not supposed to fade due to light exposure. However, it does change colour, as

ABOVE Measuring fingerboard height.

demonstrated by an experiment. A flask of madder, half covered by tinfoil and half exposed, was left in the sun, and there was indeed a definite and perceptible change in colour in the half that was exposed.

So do not leave your violin in the sun for hours on end. It will not tan but it will fade, and, what's more, it will fade unevenly, according to which areas are exposed to the sun and for how long, leaving you with an undesirable two-tone effect!

Humidity

Wood, because of its nature, absorbs water from the atmosphere. In humid environments there is more water in the atmosphere, so there is more water available for the wood to absorb and equalise. So keep your instrument away from dampness as it causes the wood to swell and change shape.

One cello turned up at our workshop in flat-pack form. The ribs had uncurled, the linings had popped off, all the centre joints had opened – basically everything that could undo had

become undone. The cause was dampness where the cello had been stored.

Very dry environments are also bad news for the same reasons. The wood shrinks as the moisture is leeched from it, and things pop open, fall off and change shape.

Fingerboard elevation

A good measure of what is going on with your instrument in terms of environmental factors is the fingerboard elevation – the angle the fingerboard makes relative to the front of the violin. Take a reference measurement and a photograph when your instrument is set up well and sounding sweet. Measure the height as shown in the photograph: all violins are slightly different but if the fingerboard is dropping under 25mm then you will have problems.

Make a habit of measuring your fingerboard elevation and check it against your reference measurement. You will even be able to start a conversation on humidity and temperature difference where you play. Some enterprising players may even want to keep a running record of the information and correlate it with local weather conditions, but perhaps this is a step too far!

The nut

You should check the nut fairly regularly, looking for abnormal wear on the nut and for string doglegs.

Nut wear

Besides assessing nut wear, also check for any pinching of the string at the nut. The cause of this is the nut becoming worn to a thin groove into which the string is pulled by tension. This is a fairly common problem, and a good example is shown in our photograph. The pinching normally occurs where the fingerboard finishes and the nut begins.

If the nut pinches, the life of the string will be shortened. The string should only sit into the groove by a quarter to one third of its width. If more than half of the string is into the groove, this can cause wear, and if this is the case then you really need to remove and replace the nut. A good test is to use a thick piece of card, such as a business card, that you can slide under the strings up against the nut – if you are unable to do this then the nut needs replacement. If the wear is not too severe, the method of repair is to remove the strings and use a fine needle file to open up the groove slightly.

Doglegs

The E and G strings should be angled slightly inwards and the A and D strings are straight. With the strings on, you will be able to see doglegs quite easily.

ABOVE A pinched nut.

BELOW A doglegged nut.

BELOW Checking nut wear with a business card.

Changing a string

If you decide that you need to change a string, you should be aware that even this simple process can damage a violin.

Before doing anything, put a soft folded cloth underneath the tailpiece between the front of the body and the tailpiece. The reason is that under the tailpiece you have the ball-ends of the strings, and sometimes the tuning mechanisms too. If you accidently knock the bridge there is a real danger of the tailpiece crashing down on the front of your instrument, with violent contact between hard metal bits and nice spruce. So to guard against this, packing under the tailpiece will provide protection to the front.

If you need to change an E or G string, you may find that other strings cross over it in the peg box. The best way to deal with this is to loosen off these strings and move them to one side with tweezers before removing the E or G string.

When changing a string, it is wise to put a little graphite into the nut groove before you fit the new string. If the other strings are loose, these can be done at the same time. The graphite prolongs the life of the strings because it reduces the friction – and hence wear – of the string on the nut. A 9B pencil, which can be bought from an art shop, will provide you with a handy source of graphite; simply sharpen the pencil and rub it into the groove.

BELOW Packing a tailpiece to protect the wood.

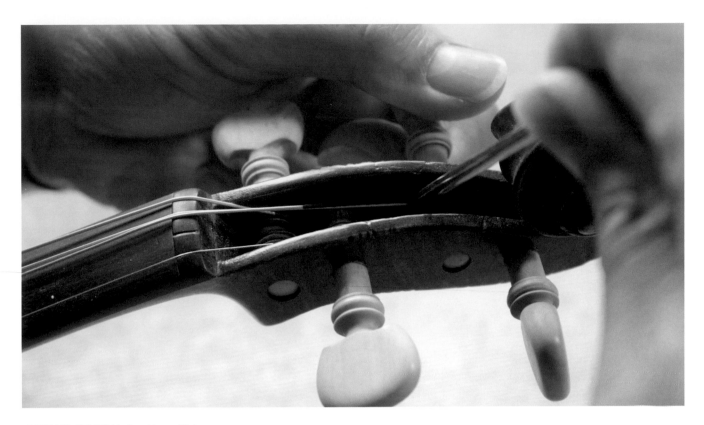

ABOVE AND BELOW Moving strings with tweezers.

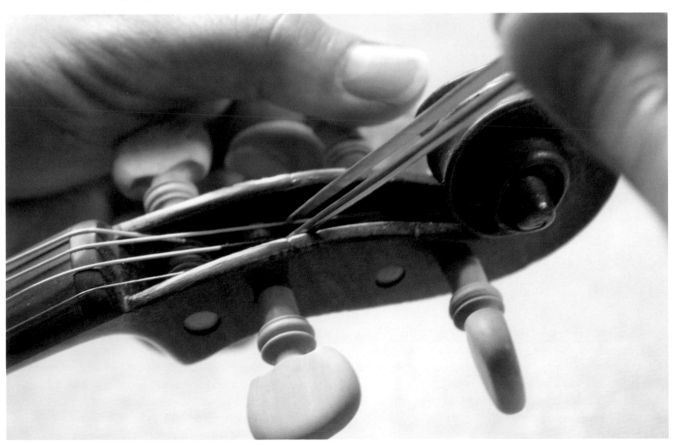

De-stringing the instrument

If you want to change the tailpiece or change the nut, or replace all the strings, then you need to de-string your instrument. If you follow these steps, you will not harm your instrument. If you go at it too enthusiastically you can cause yourself a lot of unnecessary difficulty. If at all possible, try to avoid taking off all the strings at the same time.

1 **Recording your set-up** Before doing anything, you need to record where everything is. Take a white watercolour pencil and get it to a sharp point. Dab the tip in water to activate the pencil, and put tiny marks where your bridge is sitting on the front of the violin, as shown in the photograph. These marks will help you relocate the bridge when you are setting up again. You should also take a thin flexible rule, and gently put it through the f-hole on the treble side until it touches the sound post. Take the measurement of where the sound post is located, just in case the sound post falls down as you release the string tension (if this happens you may want to refer to the section on setting the sound post).

2 **Chin rest removal** If there is a chin rest on the instrument, you need to identify what kind you have. Chin rests have keyholes for the little screws that clamp on to the instrument. If the chin rest has keyholes going all the way through, then be *very* careful with the key. As seen in the photograph, the key can protrude through the other side and scratch the rib wood as you undo the screws.

3 **Tailpiece packing** Place the packing under the tailpiece as described in the section 'Changing a string'. You can take off the middle strings first, leaving the E and G strings in place.

4 **String removal** Slacken the E and G strings and then carefully remove the bridge. Pop all the pieces into a little bag to avoid losing any of them.

5 **Awareness** Once string tension is off, the sound post may fall over. You need to get the sound post back up again and this can be a tricky task. However, if you follow the instructions in this book (see Chapter 6, 'Intermediate maintenance') you can become competent at setting your own sound post.

6 **Fitting new strings** If your tailpiece has a fine tuner, make sure you unwind this so that it can be used when the violin is strung up. If it is wound to the end, then you will have no adjustment in your fine tuner. Do not overly unwind the tuner as it may fall out. Put the ball end of the string into the tailpiece, and feed the string up and into the hole in the peg; it helps to bend the end of the string over to feed it through the hole. Turn the peg towards the scroll and wind the string, maintaining tension, and tune up as normal.

Some additional tips

When going on a journey with an instrument, it is safe for it to travel strung up if it will be with you all the time. However, if an instrument is being shipped for any reason, careful measurements should be taken, the bridge and sound post taken down, and the strings removed – all as described above.

If you have to de-string the instrument, knock over the sound post before moving it anywhere. There are two ways you can do this: you can use a sound post setter, or a flexible ruler, through the treble f-hole; another method is to gently squeeze the sides of the instrument so that the pressure lifts the front enough for the sound post to fall over.

Pegs

Two things can happen to pegs: they stick and become hard to turn, or they undo too quickly and will not hold the tune of the instrument.

If you have trouble with pegs that will not hold, try pushing the peg more firmly into the hole on the final turn as you are tuning the violin. Before you do, though, have a good look at the peg box to make sure there are no cracks on the peg holes, as a bit too much force may cause a lot of damage, and even result in the top of the scroll coming off! The hole for the A peg is particularly vulnerable as the grain is shorter here.

If the peg still will not hold, check that it fits satisfactorily in the hole. With the peg firmly seated, grip the peg with your fingers and see if you can hold up the violin at an angle, with the bottom bout tilting towards you slightly. If the peg holds the violin's weight, you know that the peg will hold under tension from the string. Make sure you do this over something soft in case you accidently drop the violin!

RIGHT Holding up the violin by a peg.

ABOVE AND RIGHT A clicking peg can have uneven roundness corrected by sanding.

These are the products required for basic maintenance of pegs:

- **Graphite crayon or 9B pencil** Use a graphite crayon or a very soft graphite pencil to work graphite on to the peg to stop it sticking.
- **Hill's peg paste** Described by the maker as 'W.E. Hill composition for pegs that have ceased to run smoothly'.
- **Dressmakers' chalk** Used on slipping pegs, this is very soft to the touch – do not use hard blackboard chalk.

Sticking pegs

Pegs that stick and click are a common problem. If a peg makes clicking sounds when turned, it needs lubrication (with peg paste) or adjustment, or both.

To check whether a peg needs adjustment, you can employ the lip test. Push the peg into the hole and turn it vigorously ten times to build up some heat. Remove the peg and run it along the top of your lip to feel if there is even warmth. Your lip is very sensitive to temperature and is probably the only part of your body you want to use to detect differences in heat in violin pegs. The peg touches the peg box in two places; you will be able to detect which of these areas is warm.

If there is uneven warmth, take a small strip of 400-grit wet-and-dry paper and run it round the peg side that is warmer, just to take off a small fraction. Do not sand the whole peg – just where the peg is warmer and shiny.

After sanding, try fitting it again, reheat, and repeat the lip test. If it turns out that the peg is completely off, no amount of

BELOW Products for pegs.

BELOW Applying peg paste.

gentle sanding will work. You will probably need to take your instrument to a professional violin maker or dealer to have new pegs fitted.

If the pegs are running satisfactorily, and you have even amounts of warmth after the lip test, all you need to do is apply graphite to each peg where it touches the peg box.

First of all apply graphite to the peg, then insert it in its hole and work it around vigorously, clockwise and anti-clockwise. The best approach is to use one hand for one direction and then switch hands for the other direction, to save your fingers and wrists from strain. Turn the peg around 10 to 20 times to ensure that the graphite is worked well in and evenly distributed.

The next step is to apply peg paste. Remove the peg again and apply a small amount of paste to the same touching points, and repeat the process. If you apply too much peg paste, it is not a problem as it just works off as you rotate the pegs. The peg paste helps to hold the graphite or chalk in place.

At each step check the peg movement in the hole to see if there is still clicking. If the pegs still stick, add more graphite and repeat the process.

Slipping pegs

If a peg slips and will not hold the string tension, we do not use graphite but instead use chalk followed by peg paste. The remedy is to repeat the process described in 'sticking pegs', working chalk into the peg. The chalk improves the grip of the peg in the peg hole.

Take the pegs out to check for uneven wear in the form of shiny areas on the peg shank. Sometimes the shank goes oval,

ABOVE Applying chalk to a slipping peg.

which can happen with ebony as this wood takes such a long time to season. A new peg may have been fitted properly, but the wood can change and become oval as it fully seasons – but only seasoned wood should be used to start with.

You may need to use a small needle file and sandpaper to correct this problem and make the peg circular again. If in doubt about doing this, take the peg to a violin specialist with your diagnosis.

You may see that a peg is not touching at all in some places, with no sign of shine on the shank. This can sometimes happen with old instruments, where the peg has just been jammed in and not fitted properly. If this is the case, take your instrument to a violin dealer or restorer and let them assess the problem.

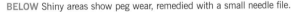

BELOW Shiny areas show peg wear, remedied with a small needle file.

Tailpiece

There are several kinds of tailpieces available to suit taste and requirements. Tailpieces can be made of wood, metal or plastic, and have built-in fine adjusters or you can fit adjusters yourself. Some players prefer just one adjuster, for the E string. With only one adjuster, all tuning must be done with the pegs, but with fine adjusters you can make slight tuning adjustments across the board. Adjusters can be attached to the tailpiece or be integral with it.

The important thing to note with the tailpiece is its precise position relative to the bridge. The distance from the bridge to where the string is secured in the tailpiece needs to be one-sixth of the distance from the bridge to the nut. The reason is that there is a harmonic relationship between the two lengths of the string separated by the bridge, and this 1:6 ratio is important for tone. If the ratio is off, the tone will be off. So, measure the bridge-to-nut length of the string, divide by six, and that will be the bridge-to-tailpiece length of the string.

Tail gut

Tail gut normally comes with the tailpiece nowadays, but you can buy it separately at specialised shops and different materials are available.

The underside of the tailpiece has two brass screws or winders. If you remove one of these you can feed the tail gut through the tailpiece and back on itself, and then secure the brass ring back. Then you need to adjust the length of the tail gut to get the 1:6 ratio.

ABOVE Brass screws in a tailpiece.

Due to stretching, allow the instrument to rest for a full day after tuning before making final adjustment of the tail gut.

Once you have the tail gut in place, you can cut it back, and warm the ends with a match and dab the ends back to form a mushroom shape, which locks the adjusters of the tail gut in place, preventing it from working loose.

ABOVE, RIGHT AND BELOW Cutting back the tail gut, warming an end with a match, and dabbing the end to form a mushroom shape.

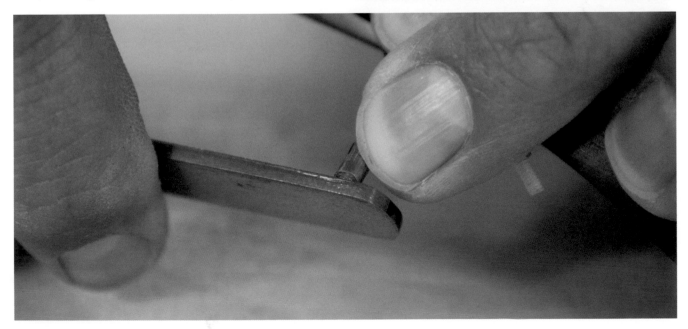

Sound quality

The quality of sound that emanates from your instrument can be influenced by many factors, including those bound to the skill of the player! If your instrument has sounded good in the past but now sounds like it needs help, this section describes the things to check.

Cracks

Visually inspect the instrument for cracks and examine old cracks that may have opened up. If you suspect an open crack, use a little water on the crack and flex the plate very gently; if the crack is open the water will be drawn in. If that happens, clean around the crack with a cotton bud, and wipe a tiny amount of hot animal glue into the crack. Before the glue sets, make sure you wipe off any excess glue with a damp tissue or cloth as it can damage the varnish.

BELOW Tapping to check all plates are closed.

Plates

Before you do anything, check that all the plates are closed. Rap gently with the knuckle of a ring-free index finger and tap. You will hear a rattle if you hit the plate where it is open. In some cases the sound deteriorates if a plate comes away from the ribs and can be punctuated by buzzing noises when playing.

Bridge position

With all the tuning that goes on, sometimes the bridge can go for a little walk. Its position can shift slightly and become disconnected from the sound post area. This is a critical position

THIS PAGE A leaning bridge, and returning a bridge to its correct position.

for the bridge, and deviation from this location can really affect how the instrument sounds, as well as its power and presence.

If you suspect a wandering bridge, take a few measurements to see if it is where it should be. Measure where the sound post is with the gauge, the template for which can be found in the back of this book. Check this is in the correct position in relation to the bridge.

The bridge may also be pulled forwards by the strings and not be in proper contact with the violin. If this happens, you can easily remedy the situation by gently pulling the bridge upright again.

Strings

Strings do not last forever, so if you have not replaced your strings in a while, try a nice new set. Be careful to follow the de-stringing procedures outlined earlier in this chapter. It is also a good idea to be competent with the sound post setter before you completely de-string the instrument, just in case the sound post falls over.

Sound post

The position of the sound post may not be correct. If you measure the position with a sound post gauge and find that it has moved, you can return it to its correct position by gently tapping it with the sound post setter.

Before moving or setting a sound post on your cherished instrument, you might want to practise first on a cheap instrument to build up confidence and skill. It would be a good idea to actually buy a very cheap instrument for practice. If you knock over the sound post when doing it 'for real' and are unable to stand it back up, you will need to take your instrument to a professional.

Even if the sound post is in the correct position in terms of measurement, this may not be the ideal position for the instrument. Adjusting the position of the sound post is an experimental process, so move it in small increments, perhaps just 1mm at a time, and judge whether the sound improves.

Before moving the sound post, mark the position of the bridge with a watercolour pencil, and use the sound post gauge to mark the position of the sound post too. Slacken the strings, and then you can make your position adjustment. Then tighten the strings, retune and play.

It is a good idea to have help from a friend or relative with a good ear, because what you hear up close to the instrument might be different to what other people hear. If you do not have a handy helper, you could try recording yourself each time you make an adjustment and keep a note of what you did for each recording.

We close this chapter with some sound post tips:

- Move it towards the E for a brighter E, or towards the G for a brighter G.
- If the E is too bright, you might want to move the sound post away from the E.
- If the instrument lacks power, move the sound post towards the bridge.
- If you want a softer sound, move the sound post away from the bridge.
- You *must* slacken the strings before moving the sound post, otherwise you could damage the instrument.

BELOW Tone control.   **BELOW RIGHT** Power control

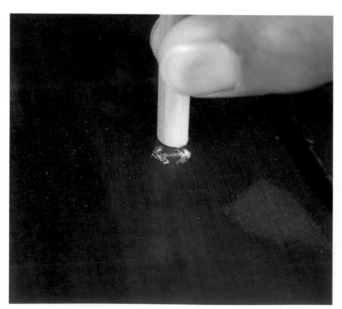

Bow bug

Bow bugs are little critters that like eating bow hair. The larvae of a beetle, they can inhabit violin cases and dine on your newly rehaired bow with great gusto. This may cause your bow hair to become brittle or break during playing. They are otherwise harmless creatures, and your violin case can make a comfortable home for them, especially if you kindly feed them your bow and leave them there in the dark. Bow bugs are small and difficult to see, partly because they hide in the cracks in your case when you try to find them.

If you think you have bow bugs then you need to take these steps:

- Cut the hair off the bow and dispose of the hair.
- Thoroughly vacuum your case, getting into all the cracks.
- Ventilate your case: leave it open so that air and light can get to it (bow bugs like dark places).
- Pop some mothballs in the case and leave it for a few weeks.
- Test for cleanliness by putting some bow hair bait in the case and leaving it for a few weeks. If the hair is damaged, you still have the problem and you should probably dispose of the case.

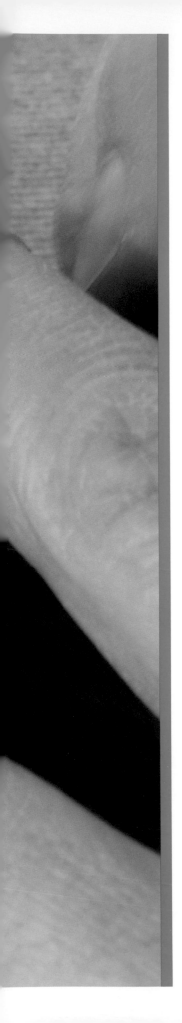

CHAPTER 6

Intermediate maintenance

Maintenance techniques at this
level are more complex than
those covered so far.
We recommend you try these
out on a cheap instrument
until you are confident enough
to work on something better.

Glue

If you have to stick something back together you will need glue. It is essential to adhere to violin-making tradition and experience and use animal glue, which is a natural adhesive product made from collagen, the proteins of which form a molecular bond with the glued surface.

Among the different qualities of glue, rabbit-skin glue is considered the best for violin work because it is light-coloured and can be one of the strongest glues. Animal glues may also be called hide glue or scotch glue.

Materials and equipment

Animal glue is inexpensive and available in granule or powder form; the powder form melts more evenly. A 500g bag of glue will last a long time unless you are doing a lot of restoration work.

The equipment you need for gluing is all very simple, as follows:

- Jam jar or glue pot.
- Baby warmer, or saucepan with marbles.
- Glue brushes, large and small – these can be ordinary artists' brushes.
- Hairdryer – handy for pre-warming the surface to be glued and to apply heat if the glue begins to set prematurely.
- Kitchen towel.

BELOW Glue equipment.

Properties of animal glue

Unlike synthetic glues, animal glue is derived entirely from animal products and has some very important properties, as follows:

- **Reversibility** Animal glue is completely reversible. If you make a mistake when joining two pieces, it is much easier, compared with other glue products, to separate them and reglue them. This is very important in the restoration and repair of instruments where parts may need to be removed and reset. Unlike PVAs and epoxies that are impossible to separate cleanly, animal glue does not disrupt the glued surfaces, preserves the original woods and materials, and can be removed with a little hot water.
- **Colour** Animal glue is generally colourless, and will not stain the materials it bonds.
- **Stability** Animal glue is very stable over time, as countless centuries-old instruments will attest, and is unaffected by solvents such as varnish and cleaning products. It also continues to work even after it has dried, pulling the joint together as the water leaves the glue. Note that animal glue is hygroscopic, so it will reabsorb moisture from the environment.
- **Strength** Animal glue is very strong, and forms a very good bond as it cools. Animal glue is used in 'rub joints', which are made with no clamp pressure, and works purely on the strength of the glue and the quality of the join of the glued surfaces. The strength of the glue can be altered by the amount of water mixed with it; this is helpful for temporary gluing of items such as studs. Sometimes glue can get stronger as it is cooked, but eventually repeated cooking of glue will lessen its ability to stick.
- **Non-toxic** Animal glue is non-toxic – its fumes and substance are benign. The only hazard can come from the heating of it, simply because care needs to be taken with any hot substance.

Preparation of glue

This step-by-step sequence takes you through the procedure for preparing animal glue to exactly the right consistency.

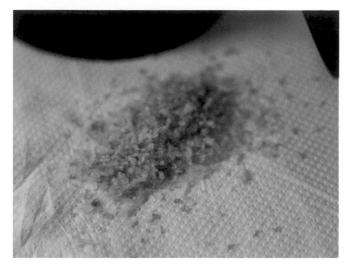

1 Place an amount of glue in a glue pot. You can use a clean jam jar for this, but we should point out that a jam jar will have a limited life in the thermal environment to which we subject it, and if it is used repeatedly the bottom may fall out while being heated.

2 Pour in enough water to cover the glue granules, and then swill the jar around so that all the granules are equally coated in water. If you do not do this, the granules at the top will soak up the water and those at the bottom will stay dry. Avoid leaving a puddle of water on top of the glue, so you can see the consistency of the glue as it melts.

3 Heat the glue on the stove in an old saucepan filled with water. A water-bath arrangement works best for glue making and you can achieve this by placing marbles in the bottom of the saucepan, so that there is no direct heat on the bottom of the jar. Place the jar in the pan, with the lid off, and with the water surrounding the jar above the level of the glue, so that the glue is surrounded. Do not heat the water over 65°C because higher temperatures destroy the glue proteins and the glue will not work. An alternative to this arrangement is a baby's milk warmer. This has the added benefit of maintaining the glue at a constant temperature, but the warmer can get clogged up with glue if you dip your brush in the water bath and it is a pain to clean.

4 As you heat the glue it will begin to melt and you can check the consistency with a brush. When the glue is melted and gloopy, you can add more hot water and mix. Always use hot water and add in *small* amounts until the required consistency is gradually achieved. If you add too much water, do not try to compensate by adding more glue granules as this does not work very well – just cook off the excess water and be patient.

5 Test with your fingers to check if your glue is ready. The glue will be hot, but it will not burn your fingers if you have not overheated it. Put a small amount of glue on your thumb and press your forefinger to it, hold for 60 seconds, and see how tacky it feels when pulling them apart. If you can easily pull your fingers apart, the glue is not ready. If the glue pulls then it is probably ready. If you fall asleep and leave your fingers together for a few hours they will stick together, but should this ever happen just use hot water to free them.

6 You can also test glue consistency with a substantial brush of at least 1cm thickness. Dip the brush in the glue pot, hold it above the pot and observe the glue flow:

- If the glue flows off the brush in a continuous stream but with lumps, it needs more water.
- If the glue falls in a straight, even flow, then you have the strongest glue as used by violin makers for super-strong joints.
- If the glue flows with breaks, this is a thinner consistency that is suitable for repairing cracks.
- If the glue runs off like water droplets, it contains too much water, so evaporate off the water until it is the correct consistency or use it for glue sizing.

7 Keep the glue warm and it is ready to use.

We have two further tips to pass on. To make the very best, strongest glue, soak the glue granules overnight in water, then heat the mixture the next day. For better strength and consistency, cook the glue twice.

Be careful when preparing hot glue as you are dealing with a potentially hazardous, hot, fluid, sticky substance. At normal working temperatures it will not burn you, but if you overheat it, or it splashes in your face, it could cause injury.

If you spill hot glue on the floor, take care to wipe it up. If you leave it, then it will tend to set with an almost frictionless, glass-like surface, and will conduct you rapidly from an upright position to the recumbent should you slip on it.

Finally it must be mentioned that we are dealing with animal products, and the somewhat pungent aroma is an acquired taste, though not toxic.

Preparing surfaces for gluing

Before gluing a surface, make sure it is clean and free from dust and shavings. If you are repairing a crack, you only need to make sure the crack is clean, as the fibres in the crack will bond back together when glued.

If you are making an instrument, the surfaces that are to be glued must be very smooth and clean to ensure a good bond. To prepare a surface, make sure it is planed flat, or made flat with a sharp chisel. Do not use sandpaper, as this tends to clog the pores of the wood and can leave a residue that does not stick very well.

Gluing the surfaces

Always do your gluing in a warm, draught-free area, and make sure that nobody is going to walk in on you, open a window or create other inconvenience (cats can be particularly good at this). The reason for this is that the glue works on a thermal basis, so draughts can speed up the cooling time and reduce the glue's working time.

Before gluing anything, have a dry run. This helps you see where everything will go. Make sure things will fit, and make sure that you have all the equipment you need, such as clamps. It also helps you determine if you are going to have any problems, such as how to hold the work. It is also helpful during the dry run to mark with a pencil where you place clamps. A little preparation will allow you to work faster when under the stopwatch of glue-setting time.

Get some glue on the brush, and wipe the excess into the glue pot. Quickly brush the glue evenly over the surfaces to be glued and press together. You can apply pressure using a clamp. Wipe off excess glue with some hot water and clean kitchen towel and aim for clean and tidy work.

You have a little working time with the glue depending on the temperature and speed at getting it on to the gluing surfaces. You can tell when the glue is setting, as it turns to a jelly-like consistency. At this point it is no use trying to move things around and make them stick – always work with hot, fluid glue.

Leave the piece to cool and dry. If it is to be a super-strong joint, leave it for at least eight hours for the glue to properly set. Simpler joints will be ready to work in about four hours.

When it goes wrong

When it goes wrong, do not panic. Remember, you are using animal glue, which is completely reversible and relatively easy to remove.

If your joint does not work, here are some of the reasons:
- You did not cook the glue enough – check the consistency of the glue before you use it.
- Glue has a limited active life – it can only be reheated and reused so many times before it loses its effectiveness. Similarly, it has a limited shelf life, and should be discarded after a week or so if unused.
- You added too much water – this comes down to the consistency of the glue. If you add too much water, you need to cook it off or start again, which is quicker.
- The glue set before you had finished working – as the glue cools it gels, and it is at this point that it becomes less good at sticking things. Make sure you work quickly enough.
- The surfaces were not well prepared – if the surfaces to be bonded are not a good fit, the joint will be weak and may not work at all. Animal glue does not fill gaps very well. Before gluing, make sure that you prepare and clean your surfaces well, and that they fit together well.

Storing glue

Another helpful feature of animal glue is that it can be kept in its mixed form. After you have finished using it, balance a lid on the pot and allow it to cool. When the pot has cooled you can screw on the lid, but do not try to do this while the pot is hot. The glue can be reused for up to a week, depending on how often you reheat it. Store the glue in a dry place away from windows. With each reheating it can lose some of its initial stickiness, so be sure to do the strength test with your fingers to see if it is still viable.

Removing glue

To remove recent glue, just use hot water and plenty of paper towels. The glue will partially dissolve in the hot water and allow you to move the parts or open the gaps. If removing glue from a crack, just work the hot water into the crack, flexing the crack to draw in the water. If the glue is very strong, you can lay undyed cotton along the crack to soak it open.

Water does not work so well on very old glue. In this case you can use methylated spirit, which works pretty well. Methylated spirit causes the glue to crack, and fail, so you need to make sure you target the area you are ungluing. A good way to do this is to run methylated spirit down a parting knife blade into the joint you are working on, and you will hear the glue cracking. A word of warning: be careful when using methylated spirit as this also tends to dissolve varnish efficiently!

Glue sizing

You can use glue to 'size' a surface. This stabilises the wood and prepares it for gluing. You size a surface by brushing on a thin layer of glue and allowing it to dry. It is especially helpful to size end-grain, because it soaks up water and glue quickly, and if you neglect to do this you can end up with dry joints because the glue gets sucked up into the wood. Sizing prevents this from happening by creating an impermeable barrier to glue moving through the wood.

Glue sizing is also helpful when cutting f-holes as the stabilised wood offers a more consistent feel to the knife than if the wood were cut without glue.

Sound post

The best sound post material is 6–6.5mm diameter close-grained spruce, ideally with six or seven lines of grain across the wood.

If the post is fitted too tightly, tone will suffer. Furthermore, a tight sound post can cause a nasty crack in the front of the violin, called, unsurprisingly, a sound post crack. If this happens the front will have to come off, and the problem patched.

If the sound post is too loose, it may fall over and render the violin unplayable – and this is not a good thing to happen if you have the strings on. If the sound post is not set correctly, it will also affect tone and will eventually fall over. With strings off, you can remove the end pin and look into the violin to see the position and orientation of the sound post – if it is leaning it is not set correctly.

Minor adjustments to the position of the sound post are covered in the 'Sound

LEFT A sound post and a bridge.

BELOW A bridge.

quality' section in the previous chapter. Now we will look at what happens if you need to replace or reset the sound post.

The basics of resetting a sound post

If the sound post falls over inside the violin you will need to get it back into position again. If the sound post is up you can induce it to fall over, by gently tapping it with the sound post tool, or gently squeezing the C-bouts of the violin with your hand. The pressure of your hand on the side of the violin lifts the front slightly, allowing the sound post to drop.

You first need to get the sound post out of the violin. If you turn the instrument upside-down you will hear the post rattling around inside. You need to manoeuvre it until it is near an f-hole, and it will probably just drop through at that point. You can then inspect it and see if you need a new post. You might need a new sound post if the old one is not a good fit – either because it keeps falling over or is putting too much pressure on the front and back plates – or if it is so riddled with sound post tool holes that it looks like it has been in a mini knife fight.

If there is no reason to fit a new sound post, put the old one back using a special tool called a sound post setter. These are cheap, and come in various designs. One end is usually

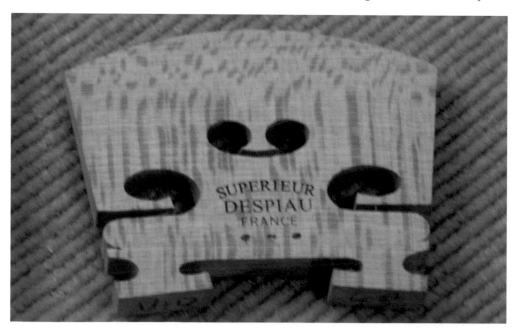

sharpened to a point, while the other has a variety of shapes designed to manoeuvre a sound post around. When you purchase a new sound post setter, the stem will need to be bent to shape – this is a very personal tool and the bent shape will somewhat resemble the curvature of an f-hole – and you will also need to sharpen the tip.

The tools and materials required for resetting a sound post are as follows:

■ Sharp chisel with a wide blade, some prefer a knife.
■ Fine saw.
■ Bench hook.
■ Sound post gauge.
■ Watercolour pencil.
■ Flexible rule.

In the following sections we will first look at the mechanics of getting a sound post into the violin, and then we will look at positioning it correctly with respect to the bridge.

Inserting a sound post

The first thing to do is to rest your violin on its back on a piece of old carpet. If you can secure the violin it helps when you are a novice because it leaves both hands free, but most craftsmen do not need to do this.

ABOVE The tools for resetting a sound post.

BELOW A sound post tool.

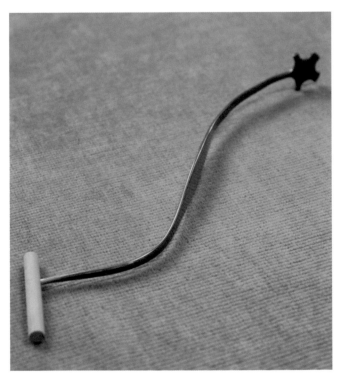

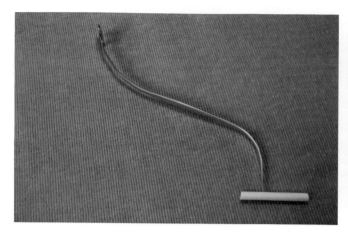

ABOVE The sound post tool set into the post.

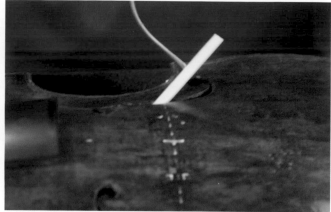

ABOVE Putting the sound post through the f-hole on the treble side.

Next you need to locate your sound post on to the tool. It should fit reasonably firmly and not dangle off when you pick up the tool. The blade end of the tool should be sharp, and you will probably find a convenient hole in the sound post – normally at one end of it – that was used by the last setter. This may help you figure out which way up the sound post is supposed to be, as the ends of the sound post are shaped to fit the slightly differing front and back curvature profiles of the relevant areas inside the violin.

Next, pass the sound post through the f-hole on the E-string side of the violin. The widest point of the f-hole is the notched area in the centre of the f-shape. If you happen to try the other f-hole you will quickly find that you hit the bass bar. Take great care with the sound post setter through the f-holes as the wood can be dented easily, and this will spoil the look of the violin – sometimes in auction display you will see cases of 'sound hole abuse'.

Now comes the tricky part. You need to pop the sound post in between the back and front plates inside the violin, so that it sits comfortably without falling over. This comes with practice, but do not be disheartened if it takes a while to master. You need to train your fine motor controls in the hand wielding the sound post so as to be sufficiently dextrous with the setter, to avoid damage to the f-holes, to pop the sound post delicately into position, and then to detach the tool from the post without pulling it down again.

You will find the distance between the back and front inside the violin varies with the arching, so there will be some areas where the sound post fits snugly and others where it will not fit at all and just falls over. With the violin lying flat on its back, insert the sound post through the treble-side f-hole, bring it to the upright position, and then pull it – using the shaped end of the setter – towards you and towards the f-hole through which it entered. As the arching of the violin drops down towards the edge, the sound post will at some point lodge neatly. Another gentle pull towards you will release the setting tool, leaving the sound post upright. In practice

your first attempt is almost bound not to work and you will find yourself fishing the sound post out again.

It is good to practise on a cheap instrument, so you can get a feel for it, and you can learn to be careful with the setter and avoid damaging the f-holes. You will either find inner peace when setting a sound post or decide that the task is best passed to someone else. Keep calm and persevere and you will get better at it, but do not expect to be a natural.

Checking position

Now that the sound post is in place, you will want to check its position relative to the bridge, and see that you have got it upright. If you look through the end-pin hole you can again check the orientation of the post to see if it is leaning.

We will use our sound post tool template to check the position of the post. Gently put one strip side into the violin via the f-hole until it touches the sound post. The top part of the template will lie where the sound post is relative to the bridge position. If you have marked the bridge position with a watercolour pencil

BELOW Locating the position of the sound post relative to the bridge.

before removing it, this will help you see exactly the relationship between the sound post and the bridge foot.

Hopefully, if you have not been driven mad, you will have become competent at getting the sound post in and out of the violin and moving it around with the setter tool. Finally, try to get the grain lines of the sound post to face across the violin, perpendicular to the grain lines of the front. If they do not, you might want to make a new sound post.

Cutting a new sound post

3 Cut the sound post to size, making sure it has a nice flat bottom. Use the bench hook and a good fine saw to cut the sound post. Try not to splinter the edge of the sound post when you cut it.

4 Go through the process of setting the sound post to get an idea of the fit.

5 Adjust the fit of the sound post by chiselling off minute slivers of wood from the top and bottom, carefully holding the sound post and chisel as shown in the photograph, for maximum control.

1 To replace a sound post you need good-quality sound post wood, which you cut approximately to size. To get an idea of the size you can pass the sound post through one of the f-holes and mark the height.

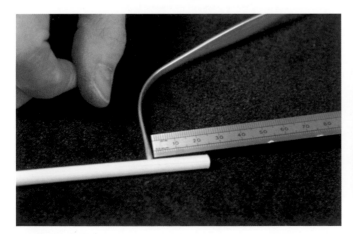

2 Fit the unfinished sound post to the tool at the right distance from one end, as shown in the photograph.

6 You do not want an uneven, bumpy surface on the ends of the sound post; the ends should be flat in the required plane for the best fit.

Bridge

If by chance you de-string your violin completely, two things can happen:

■ The sound post may fall down – this is likely.
■ The bridge will come off – this is a certainty.

This is because the tension of the strings on the bridge is what helps keep the bridge and the sound post in place. If your bridge has come off, it is the ideal time to see if it was actually in the right place, and replace it with a new one if the old one is badly fitted or worn.

The tools and materials required for bridge replacement or adjustment are as follows:

■ White watercolour pencil.
■ Templates.
■ Tape measure.
■ Flexible rule.
■ Pigment.
■ Boiled linseed oil (because it dries).

Measuring bridge position

1 With a tape measure, first determine the neck length. This is the distance from the nut to the top edge bout of the plate where the fingerboard finishes. Ideally this is 130mm but it will vary from instrument to instrument: write down what you measure, as it may not be exactly 130mm.

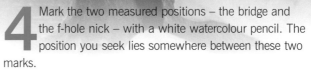

4 Mark the two measured positions – the bridge and the f-hole nick – with a white watercolour pencil. The position you seek lies somewhere between these two marks.

2 Next we calculate the middle of the bridge position along the length of the front by using this formula: ratio of neck length to body stop = 2:3. Measure the neck length, divide this measurement by 2 then multiply by 3. For example, on the instrument we are measuring the neck distance is 128mm, so: 128mm ÷ 2 x 3 = 192mm.

5 The golden rule to follow is that the bridge must be connected with the nick on the f-hole, so you can move the bridge inside these two marks. If you move the bridge beyond these marks, things do not look right and the sound will also suffer.

3 Now we reference the position of the f-hole, as this has a relationship to the position of the bridge. The treble-side inner nick in the f-hole towards the bridge is the important point to look at. If you measure the position of this nick, this should be approximate to the result of the bridge equation. In our example we measure the position of the nick to be 197mm, which differs from the result of our bridge equation – 192mm! So on our instrument there is a discrepancy – what do we do?

6 The final thing to check is the size of the bridge, and, believe it or not, this is related to the size and position of the bass bar in the instrument. As we know the bridge hinges on the sound post and transfers vibrations into the violin body, while the bass bar oscillates in counterpoint as the other bridge foot is positioned over it. On lower-grade instruments bass bars are put in with less accuracy, so the bridge may not be right for the instrument. If we take our thin flexible rule and slide it through the f-hole, it will butt up against the bass bar. We can then transfer this measurement to the top of the violin, which we will need to position the bridge. Mark the position of the bass bar edge with the watercolour pencil.

Centre-line check

You should also check the centre line. The centre line is the join between the two plates, and sometimes this is not exactly in the centre. To check the centre line, measure from the left inner purfling to the right inner purfling, across the middle of the instrument. We use the inner purfling because the outer edge of a violin may wear and distort this measurement, whereas the inner purfling will be unmoved in all but the most traumatised instruments. Purfling will have been fitted when the instrument was made, or in some poor-quality instruments carefully drawn on in ink!

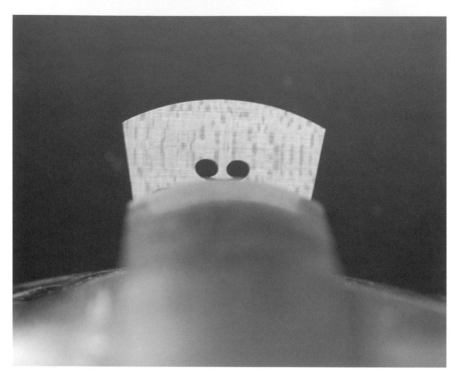

ABOVE Bridge alignment with the fingerboard.

BELOW Alignment using a bridge template.

Fingerboard alignment

Another check we should make is that the fingerboard and bridge align properly. We do this by looking down the fingerboard with one eye, and seeing where the bridge lies. It should be dead centre to the fingerboard. If it is off to one side, and you are sure of the position by the centre-line measurements, then perhaps the fingerboard is off-centre.

Bridge height

If you use the handy template from the back of this book, you can also check the bridge height. If it is too low, you need a new bridge, and it is a wonder that you could manage to play at all! If it is too high, the bridge can be adjusted by removal of material from the feet or from the top, using a very sharp knife. You only want to remove very tiny amounts and check the fit, because

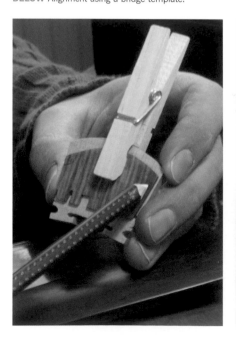

you will find that you cannot put the material back again!

A bent bridge

Due to the tension of the strings on the bridge, over time the bridge can bend. The reasons it may bend in the first place are because the medullary rays – at 90 degrees to the instrument – are not straight or the bridge is too thin. This can be a recurring problem, something that can be fixed but may then return of its own accord.

When you tune the violin, the bottom part stays put and the top of the bridge can bend. When bridges are made, they are left a little thicker in the belly, and they are shaped so that the back of the bridge is flat. The front of the bridge is curved to the top and the side, giving a little more strength to counter any bending tendency.

The first thing to ask yourself is whether or not you want to save the bridge. Perhaps the bridge needs to be replaced with one of better quality. If the medullary rays are bending towards the fingerboard, then the bridge will bend most of the time. If you decide that you must save the bridge, then follow the simple steps outlined under the heading 'Bridge Over Bubbled Water', overleaf.

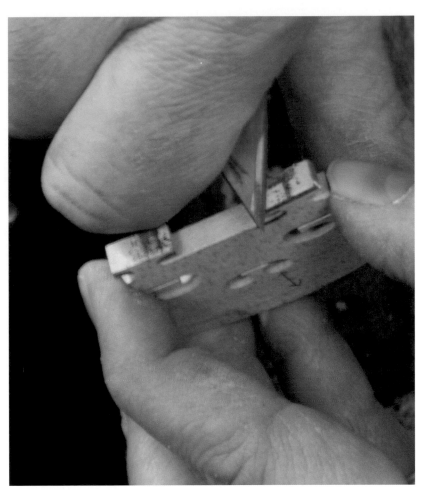

ABOVE Cutting feet.

BELOW A bent bridge before repair.

BELOW Medullary rays.

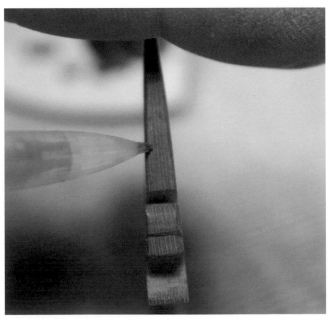

A Bridge Over Bubbled Water

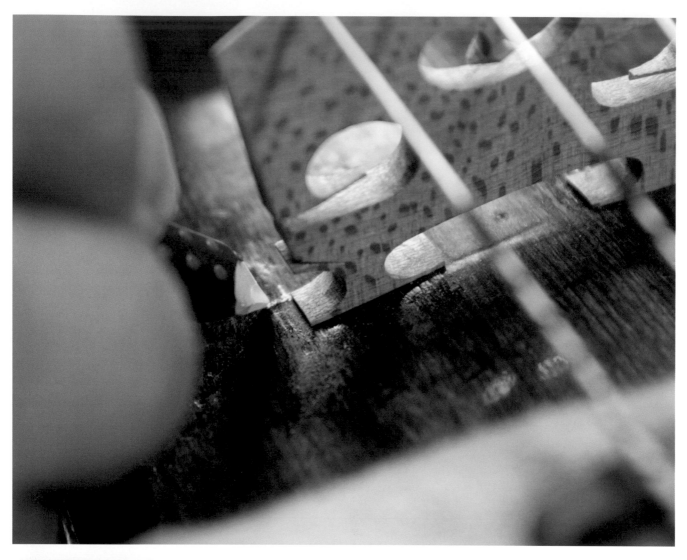

1 With a white watercolour pencil, mark the position of the bridge feet on the front of the violin.

2 De-string your instrument, following the recommended de-stringing procedure in the previous chapter of this book.

3 Remove the bridge, something that will probably happen as a matter of course as you take the strings off.

4 Prepare a cup with a teabag, with milk and sugar if you take it, and boil the kettle.

5 When the kettle is boiling, you have a steaming device at your disposal, and the means to make a nice cup of tea.

7 Clamp the bridge between two pieces of Perspex for at least three days, until it has dried.

6 Hold the bridge in long tweezers over the boiling kettle; hold the switch down on the kettle to continue the boil for a minute or so.

8 After the clamping procedure, the bridge should return to its original shape. The stamp, if the bridge has one, normally faces towards the fingerboard. The tuning process always puts pressure on the bridge to curl forwards.

Warning You are dealing with steam and artificially boiling the kettle continually. Steam will give you a nasty burn if you are not sensible, and if you boil the kettle dry the element will burn out and you will have to buy a new one. So make sure there is plenty of water in the kettle, and be careful with the steam.

Fitting pegs

If you wish to fit a new peg from scratch, you need a tool called a peg shaper. This works exactly like a pencil sharpener. The peg is placed in the shaper and rotated until the desired taper and width is created. If you are having trouble turning the peg in the peg shaper, you can apply some dry soap to the peg to lubricate it. You need to cut off the excess material from the peg and a fine Japanese saw will make a good job of this.

Scratches and dents

Scratches and dents are inevitable in a well-used instrument. Thankfully they are a minor concern and, although unsightly, are dealt with easily.

Repairing a minor ding

1 A small knock to the front of the violin can put a dent into the wood. The wood deforms under the shock, and appears as a dent. Scuffing to the varnish may also accompany the dent.

3 Next you need a hot soldering iron, hot enough to produce steam from a wet sponge. Place the hot iron on to the tissue and press lightly to produce steam. Hold the iron there for a few seconds, allowing the steam to permeate the wood.

2 The first thing to do with a dent is to try to relax the wood back to its original shape, which is done by applying heat and steam to the dent. Wet some tissue and place it over the dent.

4 Remove the tissue and check the area. If you have it right, the dent will have lifted. You may find that the wood will not relax all the way back to normal.

5 Once you have lifted the dent as much as you can, you can proceed to use clear filler such as CLOU to build up the surface if the dent still offends you. Apply this with a fine brush.

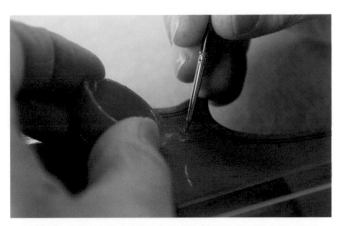

6 If the varnish is scuffed you will need to retouch it. The section 'Retouch varnish' in the next chapter gives advice on how to proceed.

7 The violin with the repair complete – pleasing to behold.

End pins

Fitting an end pin

Some makers fit and shape the end pin down to the size of the hole in the violin, but this can take a long time to do. A better method is to ream the hole in the violin, which makes it easier to fit the end pin and also gives more visibility of the sound post position should you need it.

If the hole is too big and no end pin can be found to fit, the hole will need to be bushed – the process where missing wood is replaced and shaped.

Types of reamer

When fitting an end pin, you do need an end-pin reamer. A modern professional reamer, made of high-quality steel, is designed to keep the hole round, but some people prefer the old-style German taper, which has a steeper angle and so produces a slower cut. There are two types of reamer available nowadays:

■ **Spiral reamer** With a spiral reamer you cannot really adjust the angle of the hole. If the hole is skewed and you wanted to try to correct the problem, you are better off using a flat-blade reamer.

■ **Flat-blade reamer** With this type of reamer, you can cut a portion of the circle from the hole. With control and skill you can use this method to rectify a skewed hole.

Back reaming

The modern reamer requires that you must back ream to compress the wood where you are fitting. Back reaming can actually widen the hole without cutting, because the wood is circularly compressed, and you will be surprised at how much wood will compress and how much a hole can widen in this process. The peg or end pin can drop in by 5–10mm depth. Pegs need more back reaming because they are constantly moving, so the hole on the peg should be well back-reamed.

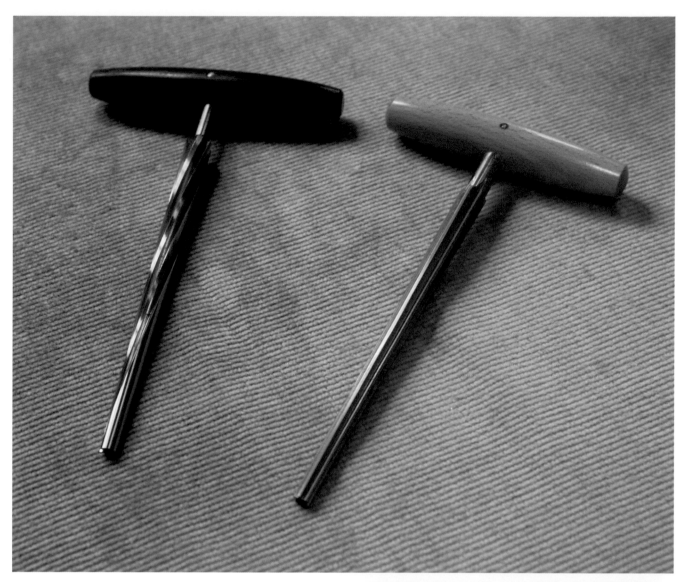

ABOVE Spiral and flat-blade types of reamer.

If the end-pin hole on the violin is skewed, you might be able to correct it by using a flat-blade reamer, but if it has become significantly off-centre then you really need to bush it.

If the end pin is a little loose, apply chalk to help it grip the hole. If it is too tight, a bit of soap may help.

You want to get the collar of the end pin sitting snugly against the ribs, but you must not force it in because that could cause a split in the bottom block, and it could be very difficult to get the end pin out again.

Bushing the end-pin hole

This process is straightforward, but we have one piece of advice. When drilling out a bushing, never drill in the centre of it as this

RIGHT Reaming the end-pin hole.

ABOVE Keep the reamer straight.

ABOVE Do not allow the reamer to go in off-centre.

will weaken the bushing and may cause it to come out. Always drill slightly off-centre as this actually helps to seat the bushing into the violin.

Ream out the end-pin hole with a peg reamer to remove any loose material.

■ Fill the hole with boxwood bushing, and glue in place.
■ Cut back the bushing carefully to the violin.

■ Retouch the bushing to the colour of the ribs.
■ Drill out the hole ready for the new end pin.

Stuck end pins

If your end pin is stuck, there are a couple of ways to deal with it. You can buy an end-pin extraction device that goes around the end pin and acts as a clamp, allowing you to pull it out. A cheaper alternative is to use a rubber mixer-tap nozzle, which gives good grip and is safe to use against the violin wood.

BELOW A snugly fitted end pin.

Peg bushing

Ebony is a much stronger wood than maple, so the years of turning the pegs when tuning do eventually cause wear to the peg holes so that the pegs no longer fit well. The answer is peg bushing.

The preferred wood for peg bushing is boxwood because it cuts nicely and you get a clean shaving in the peg reamer, helping fit. Before you start, check that there are no cracks in the peg box; if you find cracks you should seek professional help.

With a peg reamer, remove enough of the peg box inside the hole to make a clean surface all the way around – this makes it easier to fit the bushing. Also back ream the hole, using the reamer in an anti-clockwise direction, away from the cutters, in order to compress the wood.

You can buy pre-shaped bushing or you can make your own bushing from boxwood. If making your own bushing, it really needs to be done accurately on the lathe.

The first step with bushing is to drill a hole about 25–30mm from the end of the peg bush blank, allowing the insertion of a small screwdriver or Allen key; unlike a peg there is no head, so you need a way to turn the bushing. That distance needs to be about 25–30mm because the hole will break the bushing if you place it too close to the end. Try not to make the hole too big as that weakens the bushing.

Next, use the peg shaper to fit the bushing to the hole, using exactly the same method as for peg fitting, as described earlier in this chapter. The bushing must fit exactly in the hole with no gaps. It is important to align the grain of the peg bushing with the grain of the peg box because it helps blend the wood when you retouch the varnish later.

When you are happy with the fit, you can prepare the glue and brush it into the peg hole and on to the peg bushing. There is not a great deal of time before the hot glue starts to gel, so do a practice run without any glue. Push the bushing in and wind it in further so that you get a nice tight fit, then leave to dry overnight.

Once completely dry, carefully cut back the bushing flush to the peg box, taking care not to damage the peg box when doing this. Once the bushing has been cut back and trimmed flush, it should be sealed with clear shellac to prevent colour leeching into the bushing and spoiling the finish when retouching.

Finally you can drill out the bushing in preparation for fitting new pegs.

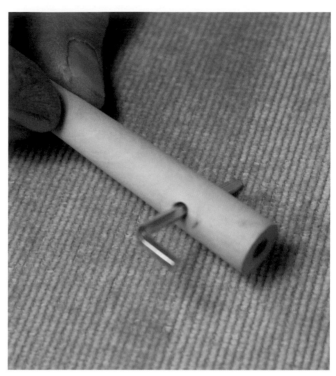

ABOVE Hole for Allen key.

BELOW Fitting the bushing.

CHAPTER 7

Advanced maintenance

The techniques described in
this section are considered to
be advanced repair methods.
These techniques are a small
cross-section of those taught at
a professional level in today's
violin making, restoration and
repair schools.

Fingerboard

The fingerboard is made of ebony, although occasionally softer woods have been used. Normally the fingerboard has a nice smooth surface because ebony is a hard wood, chosen because it is tough and wears slowly. Over time the vibration of the strings and pressure as they are pressed down on to the fingerboard cause problems.

Another way fingerboards can deteriorate is by distortion, which might cause the scoop in the fingerboard to be lost and the strings to buzz. Distortion can occur through the use of wood that has not been seasoned sufficiently and remains unstable; ebony needs a very long time to season properly and nowadays five years is considered the minimum amount of time. Wood is seasoned so that excess moisture is slowly released and the wood reaches equilibrium with its environment. During

BELOW Removing a fingerboard.

RIGHT A stained fingerboard – you
can see the hard wood coming through the
black stain.

seasoning wood can naturally change shape, split and distort,
so always make sure timber is completely seasoned before use.

To fix your fingerboard problems, you first need to de-string
the violin, and remove the nut. You can remove the nut with an
opening knife and some alcohol to dissolve the glue.

BELOW Fingerboard repairs: tools for the job.

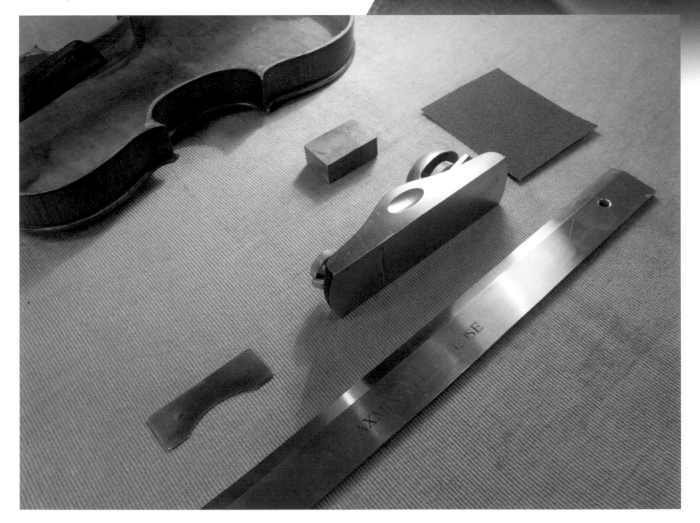

ABOVE Fingerboard scoop.

Reshooting a fingerboard

If there is a bump in the fingerboard, this can obstruct the string and cause a buzz, and the fingerboard will need 'reshooting'. As the fingerboard is not exactly flat along its length – it has a natural scoop – a small block plane is used to retain this scoop. A suitable plane is shown in one of the accompanying photographs.

A brass template, which you can make from the tool plans at the back of this book, will help you achieve the shape of the curvature of the fingerboard. The scoop is deeper on the G-string side and shallower on the E-string side.

Once the fingerboard is planed, you can use a block of wood and sandpaper to achieve the surface, working your way through the following grades of abrasive paper: 180, 240, 320, 400, 600 and 1200. Then use a fine abrasive metal polish to complete the finish.

You do need to soften the edges of the fingerboard – a player will not thank you for leaving them sharp!

BELOW A suitable block plane for working the fingerboard scoop.

BELOW Checking curvature with a fingerboard template.

Replacing a fingerboard

You may have an instrument where the fingerboard is missing, or needs replacement if it has significant wear – after years of playing the strings will wear a groove into the wood.

About 100 years ago German trade manufacture experienced a shortage of ebony, a situation that meant ebony was used only for the better-quality instruments, with other instruments using beech or fruitwood stained with ink or clothes dye. One tell-tale sign of a trade instrument is a beech fingerboard that has been stained; beech is not as durable as ebony and does not have that nice black patina. If a fingerboard needs reshooting and has been stained, you may need to restain it as you will see the lighter wood coming through. However, bear in mind that low-quality ebony will exhibit coloured grain and can be taken for another wood.

The fingerboard is designed to come off, and when manufactured it should have been glued on with hide glue to allow removal and replacement. If it has been glued on with anything else, you will need to take the instrument to a professional and have it examined, because the fingerboard-removal techniques outlined here will not work. Furthermore, you may end up damaging the neck trying to prise the fingerboard away. If in doubt take it to an expert.

Once the old fingerboard is off, you can fit a new one. You should select the best possible ebony fingerboard blank, or you may want to use an old cello or viola fingerboard. The reasons you might want to use an old fingerboard are:

ABOVE Grooves worn in the fingerboard.

■ It is friendlier to the environment.
■ It may save you a little money.
■ Lastly, and most importantly for the integrity of your violin, it will be more stable than anything you can buy new. A fingerboard from an old instrument may be 100 years old and therefore well-seasoned.

As mentioned earlier, ebony takes a long time to season, so when buying an ebony blank try to make sure that the wood has been seasoned for at least five years, and buy from a reputable source. If at all possible, keep the blank in your house for at least a year to further season it.

Sometimes a fresh fingerboard will unhappily move as you plane and work with it. As you plane you release tension in the wood, allowing the wood to adjust itself, and typically the fingerboard will banana away from the instrument, which has the effect of lowering the string height.

Like many tropical woods, ebony can have toxic effects. Ebony dust problems include dermatitis, conjunctivitis and sneezing. There are also cases of skin sensitisation induced by ebony dust. However, there are some simple precautions you can take. You should work in a well-ventilated area, or outside if the weather is fine. Wear a protective dust mask, and wash and clean your work area and yourself thoroughly after finishing work.

Fingerboard replacement

To remove the fingerboard you will only need a few tools:

- A parting knife.
- A fine brush.
- Methylated spirit.

1 Start by looking for an opening on the neck at the top (where the nut is) or the bottom where you can insert your parting knife. You need to take care now, because a parting knife is quite blunt compared with a chisel, so you end up using more force – which is where you have the potential to cause damage to yourself and the instrument. Make sure the hand holding the instrument is not in the path of the knife, because the glue can suddenly give way and all the force you have behind the knife at that point will be converted into uncontrollable kinetic energy, and you may end up cutting yourself.

2 Dab a little methylated spirit on to a brush and let it run down the knife and into the parting, being careful that none runs on to the varnish of the instrument. Allow a little time for the methylated spirit to work and eventually the glue will emit a cracking sound as it gives way.

3 Remove all residual glue from the violin neck, where the fingerboard sat, using a sharpened scraper and trying not to score or otherwise damage the wood of the neck. You can use a little water to help this removal process. Once you have completed this, you can check that the neck is flat and true, and the old glue is completely off. If the neck is not flat or has bumps in it, there is not a lot you can do about it.

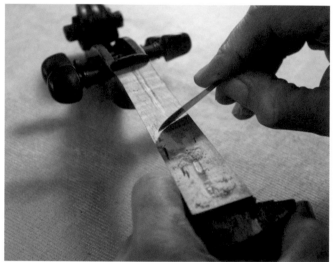

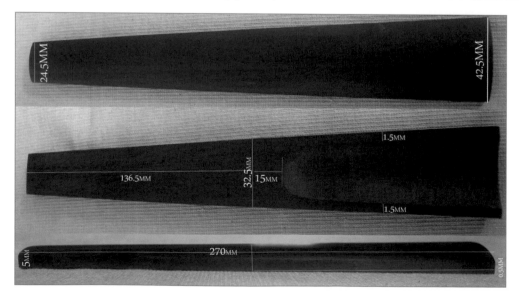

4 Taking the new fingerboard, start by flattening the underside of it, referring to the accompanying diagram for all the required measurements and dimensions. Flatten the underside with a sharp block plane.

5 Take a marking gauge and run it around the edge of the fingerboard to a 5mm height. It is better to take the weight down from the top of the fingerboard, rather than up from the bottom.

6 Measure the width of the neck of the instrument at two locations: where the end of the fingerboard was originally; and where the fingerboard leaves the root of the neck and overhangs the violin body.

7 Next, locate the middle of the neck and the middle of the fingerboard, and transfer that measurement on to the underside of the fingerboard. Allow yourself 0.5mm either side of that measurement for adjustment purposes.

8 Now measure the length of the fingerboard, and again make it a little longer so you can cut it down. You need a good saw: a Japanese micro-saw with fine teeth is a good choice as this will make a clean cut with no splintering.

9 Make sure you have the angles correct at the end of the fingerboard – use a sliding bevel to check. You can use a white watercolour pencil to mark on the ebony as best you can with the sliding bevel, and cut the length of the fingerboard. Finish the end with a fine rasp or a file, and then work through the grits of wet-and-dry paper to make a clean finish.

10 Next, find the middle of the fingerboard at the widest part with dividers, and, taking the measurements from the diagram, place white pencil marks to mark the width.

11 The underside has three points of reference per edge. Using a rule and a bradawl, join up the points and highlight the line with your white watercolour pencil.

12 Use a small block plane to plane down the sides to the line and also to scallop out the inside of the fingerboard to the right shape (refer to the diagram for the measurements). Check that the curve of the G-string side is bigger than the curve on the E-string side. Use a jig to hold

the fingerboard in place as you plane the shape. Do not put the fingerboard in the jig too tightly because you could distort it.

13 Clamp the finished fingerboard in four places along the neck, so that the fingerboard will not move around once it has been accurately centred on the violin. The best way to protect the neck from the clamps is to make counter blocks lined with cork.

14 Use animal glue to secure the fingerboard to the neck and take care not to apply too much glue. When gluing, dampen the top surface of the fingerboard with water to counteract the wetness of the glue; this helps to prevent the fingerboard from warping.

15 Start the gluing process by releasing two of the clamps and use a thin knife with hot glue underneath this part of the fingerboard. Replace these two clamps and release the other two, and once more apply hot glue underneath. Then replace the second pair of clamps, taking care to clean any excess glue off the neck. Leave for at least eight hours, preferably overnight.

16 When the glue is completely dry, use a very sharp, fine scraper to scrape down the excess of the fingerboard that you left on the side, taking great care not to touch the neck with the scraper. Finally you can burnish the ebony into the neck with a bone handle.

17 Recheck the curvature of the fingerboard as it may have changed a little during the gluing process. Use a straight edge to check this, and plane again as necessary. When planing on the instrument, plug the f-holes to prevent debris from getting inside.

18 Once you are happy with the final shape of the fingerboard, smooth the surface with wet-and-dry paper and finish off with a light abrasive polish to get a pleasing lightly glossed appearance.

19 Finally you need to replace the nut. You may be able to keep the old nut if it is in good condition and large enough, in which case you can glue it on and shape it down to the proper height. If the old nut is too small, you need a new one.

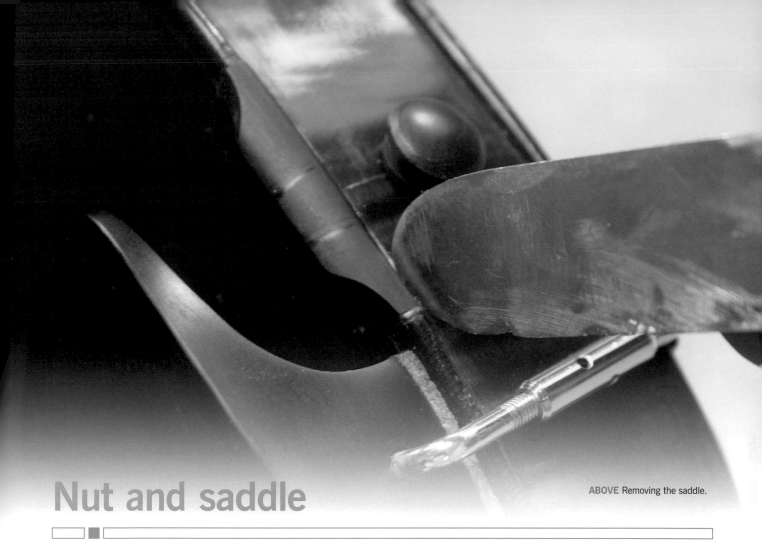

ABOVE Removing the saddle.

Nut and saddle

The nut and saddle are designed to be replaced as they get worn. Wear and tear on the nut can cause the strings to become so entrenched that they buzz horribly on the fingerboard. You may want to replace the nut if you are replacing a fingerboard so that everything is consistent.

Replacing the nut

To remove the nut or saddle you will need:

■ A palette knife or an old butter knife with a thin blade.
■ A fine brush.
■ Methylated spirit.
■ Dry soap.

1 Look for an opening between the nut and fingerboard, put some dry soap on the knife and try to work it in gently. The soap helps to lubricate the knife as it is worked into the opening.

2 Put some methylated spirit on to the knife so that it trickles down the blade into the opening, where it will gradually weaken the glue. You sometimes hear a cracking noise as the glue gives up its bond. You may have the inclination to use pressure and force, but avoid this – just wait for the methylated spirit to do its work. Safety-wise, too, you should avoid applying a lot of pressure behind a blade, in case something slips or gives. Take great care to keep the methylated spirit away from the varnish, and wipe off any excess, because spirit is very good at dissolving varnish too.

3 Sometimes during this process the fingerboard can come away with the nut. If that is the case you will need to reglue the fingerboard and then deal with the nut separately. If the fingerboard is in good condition, reglue it following the steps outlined in the previous section. If it is badly worn you might consider replacing it at this point, while the instrument is de-strung.

4 Once the nut is off, take a sharp chisel and carefully clean off the glue from the top of the neck. Do not dig into the neck: you are only interested in removing the glue and providing a clean surface for the new nut. If the glue does not come off cleanly, use warm water and tissue to revive it and then take a small scraper and scrape it off.

5 You can buy pre-shaped nuts (and saddles), which saves some work in initial shaping; we recommend you start with these. Dry-fit the nut and see what needs to be done. The nut should be flush and should not protrude into the peg box, and have a slight angle coming up from the peg box. You need to achieve flatness of the nut at the beginning of the peg box and flatness at the end of the fingerboard, with no gaps.

6 Glue the nut to the neck oversized, in both height and width. The width from fingerboard to peg box width is fitted with reasonable accuracy, whereas the other dimensions are shaped back to the violin. Mask off the area with masking tape to prevent inadvertent damage to the finish of the neck and then shape the nut in situ.

7 The shaping process is done using a chisel or knife to start with, then move to a small file to get the final shape. When the nut is nicely shaped, continue finishing with increasing grits of wet-and-dry paper; 180-grit gets rid of the file marks, and then work through 320, 400, 600 and 1200, finishing off with a fine metal polish for a nice shine. Then remove the masking tape once the nut is finished.

Retouch varnish

Retouching the original finish of a violin is a specialised art form: the objective is to create a retouch that is indistinguishable from the surrounding area under any lighting conditions.

Retouch varnish is used to replace missing varnish on a crack repair on an instrument. Layers of pigment and colour varnish are retouched on the crack and blended with the surrounding colours. The aim is to try to blend the repair so that it is indistinguishable from the original finish of the violin, including the way it follows the wood grain and any wear patterns.

The retouch is a very specialist skill, so we recommend you try it on instruments of little worth to you, in case you end up with an ugly mess.

In order to mix retouch pigment, you will need the following materials and equipment:

ABOVE An array of pigments.

- A good sable brush with a very fine tip.
- An artist's palette for mixing colours.
- A good selection of pigments.
- Tissue.
- Clear shellac.
- Filler varnish.
- Fine scrapers.
- Micromesh.

Mixing retouch pigment

ABOVE Preparing to mix pigment on a sheet of glass.

ABOVE Pigment and a Muller made of solid glass.

ABOVE Mixing pigment with spirit.

ABOVE Grinding pigment with the Muller.

ABOVE Paste-like pigment after use of the Muller.

ABOVE Scraping off the prepared pigment.

The retouching process

After a crack repair has been done, the crack is filled with shellac and built up higher than the surrounding area with filler varnish – we recommend the Deft brand. This is then very carefully cut level with a fine scraper. Coats of clear shellac are applied next, and the area gently gone over with micromesh.

If you do not fill the wood sufficiently with filler, you can get into a lot of trouble. If the pigment is allowed to come into contact with bare wood it will soak in and stain the wood.

The retouch begins with an intense pigment as a base to work from. Colours are mixed that are in sympathy with the surrounding colours of the repair area and applied. You then enter a process of colour blending, trying to achieve an invisible repair.

Let us imagine that you have mixed up the perfect colour match on the palette. If you attempt to apply this to the instrument it will not work – you need to camouflage it. A good analogy is the jungle camouflage of army fatigues – a mixture of browns, greens and blacks. If you stand in the jungle wearing this camouflage, you will blend in with the foliage because the jungle is a mixture of greens and of light and shade. If you just painted yourself green, and tried the same thing, you would find your army career cut short after the first engagement as you would stand out and get shot at!

Mix the colour using the methylated sprit as the medium to pick up the colour, but take care not to use too much spirit. The pigment tends to separate from the spirit and you end up with no colour at all on the crack, as it all pools to the side of the crack. To prevent having too much spirit in the brush, first dab the colour on to the brush, then tip the middle of the brush on to a tissue. The tissue will pull excess spirit off the brush, and leave colour pigment with enough spirit on the brush to work with. Another good reason for keeping the level of spirit down is that if you get too much alcohol on to the violin you might end up damaging the existing varnish and making things worse.

We recommend you use a sable brush with a very fine tip for maximum control and accuracy of where your colour goes. You should first look for the lightest colour you can see coming through, and retouch to that colour – this will be the background colour for the retouch. The match should be such that you are unable to see the colour going on to the instrument – if you can see the colour, you probably have too much pigment and you will have difficulty achieving a good blend.

You will find you need to change the pigment in the palette as you go. You need to have a couple of colours ready for use, and work at different places on the crack to blend the colour differences. To emphasise, this process is not about applying one colour to fill in the crack area; it is a very subtle process.

Once you have finished a blend you might then seal it with clear shellac and do another layer of colour until the work becomes indistinguishable. Some retouch work uses a

ABOVE Retouch palettes.

matting agent in the varnish to help blend the colours. You can also gently pull a finger over the retouch as another means of merging colours. Ideally you should watch an expert at work before experimenting yourself on a practice instrument.

After you have finished your masterpiece of deception, do not clean the palette; instead leave it mixed up with the colours. These exact colours cannot be bought, so you want to save them in order to be able to create further colours so that you can change the palettes slightly. In this way you can achieve a really good palette of colours that are relevant to the instruments you are retouching.

In Chapter 3 we listed the colours you may need but it is useful to repeat the list here followed by some explanatory notes:

- Orange Madder
- Indian Yellow
- Burnt Umber
- Burnt Sienna
- Lamp Black
- Prussian Blue
- Crimson Red
- Titanium White

You will use some colours in larger quantities than others. The first four listed – Orange Madder, Indian Yellow, Burnt Umber and Burnt Sienna – are used a lot in retouching. You will also use Prussian Blue quite often, but in tiny quantities; the smallest pinprick on a brush quietens down a red or orange. Of course, you will never need to mix a blue colour, but what Prussian Blue does achieve is to take away a colour's vibrancy and make it look older. Lamp Black and Crimson Red are also used to similar effect. Some retouch work can be done with dyes, as they give an intensity of colour, but be aware that dyes may not be light-fast so the great majority of the work is done with dry pigments.

You will find that it is easier to achieve a good retouch result with some finishes than with others. A particularly difficult finish to retouch is French varnish on a highly flamed back. A crack is also harder to retouch than a patch because there is no manoeuvring room.

Cracks

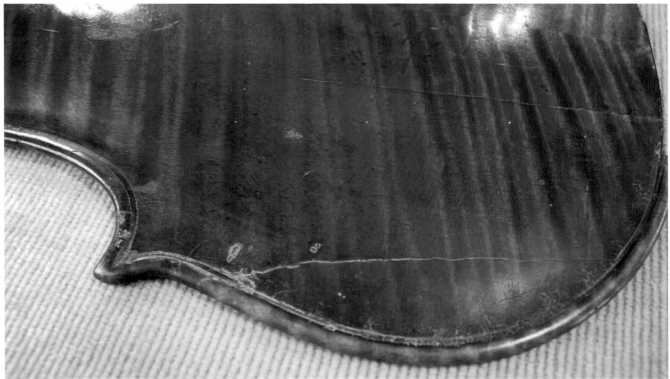

Stabilising a crack

To deal with cracks on the front of a violin, the front needs to be removed. The first thing you should do is stabilise the crack by gluing a temporary stud at the end of it. This should be chalk-fitted so that it fits well. This stud will prevent the crack from getting worse when you flex the wood open to clean the crack.

Clean the crack out with peroxide so there is no dirt in there. Once the crack is cleaned, you need to flush it out with water.

Gluing a crack

Down each side of the crack make a pencil cross every 35–40mm. Then fit small blocks of wood to the inside of the instrument either side of the crack. These studs, as they are called, are fitted so that their grain is perpendicular to the grain

ABOVE Stabilise the crack.

ABOVE Marking block positions.

ABOVE Correctly positioning blocks.　　　**BELOW** Chalk fitting.

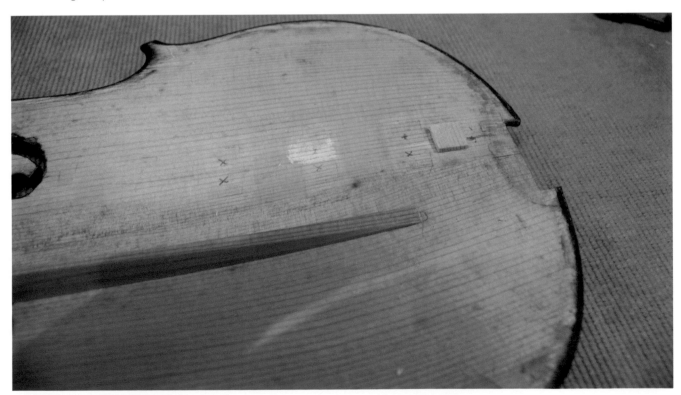

ABOVE Chalk fitting the block.

ABOVE A crack clamp.

of the front, with the end grain facing towards the crack, and they are glued at 90 degrees to each other and the crack. If you get this wrong, the process will not work. It is good practice to put a little bevel on the blocks either side of the crack, to keep glue away from the crack.

As described in the following sections, there are three

methods you can use to pull a crack together, and in some situations you may combine all three.

■ Crack clamps and wedges.
■ Perspex.
■ Stretcher clamps.

Crack clamps and wedges
You need special clamps for this job, and you need to ensure

BELOW Setting up the blocks.

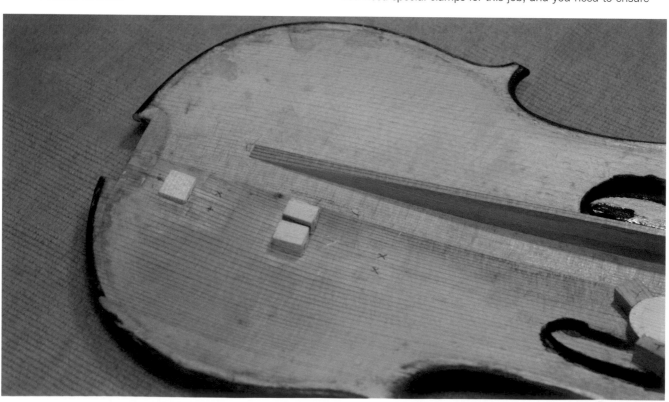

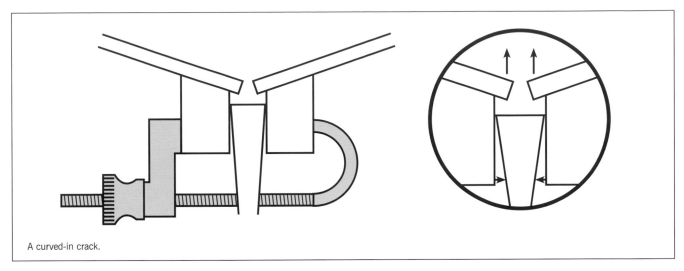

A curved-in crack.

that the blocks are not bigger than the clamps, because you do not want to cut back once they are glued. You can make the blocks a little bit longer, along the crack, but do not make them wider, away from the crack, because that will inhibit the little brass clamps.

A crack will not always go back together evenly and may want to curve in, to curve out or to step, as shown in our six diagrams. If a crack is curved in, the wedge you use needs to be a loose-fitting one, so that when you fit the clamp and apply pressure it will push the crack outwards and allow its edges to meet properly.

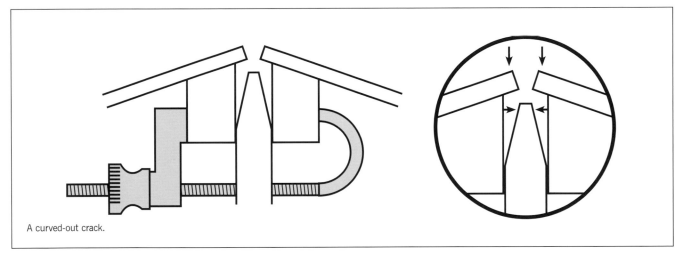

A curved-out crack.

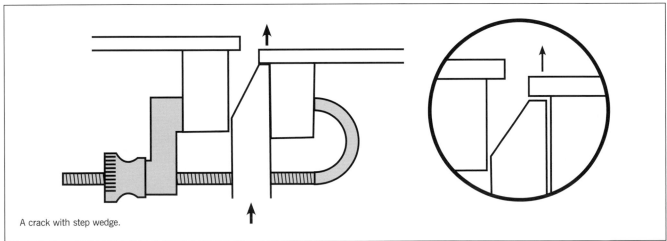

A crack with step wedge.

If a crack is curved out, the wedge you use must be tight. With a step, use a wedge with a blunt end to realign the two parts.

Do not try to glue the whole crack in one go; it is best to test the process first. To test the crack movement, you can do a dry run with hot water. Work the hot water into the crack as if you were gluing the crack, and see how the crack behaves when you apply clamping pressure. Wood can behave in unpredictable ways.

Perspex

You can place Perspex on the outside of the crack, the varnished side, to protect the front from any clamping you might do. But Perspex can flatten the area over the crack or you can get a line dug in from the Perspex, so to stop either of these possibilities you can use two pieces of Perspex layered on top of each other.

LEFT AND BELOW Using wedges.

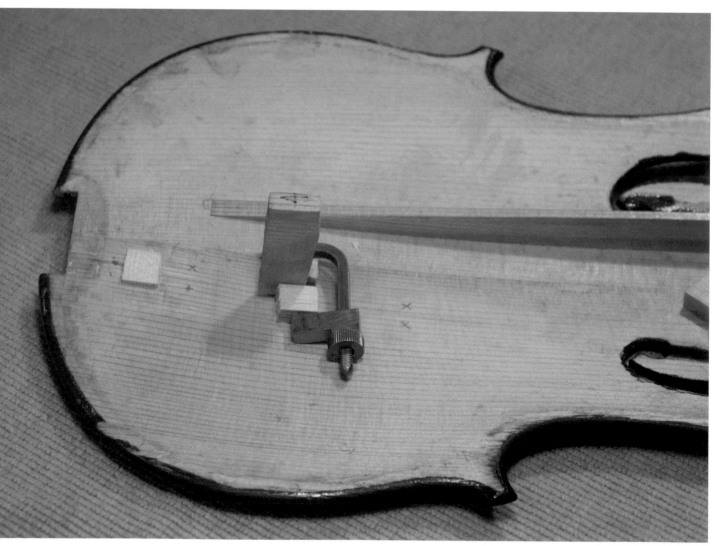

The uppermost piece is fatter than the lower piece, which helps to dissipate the pressure from the clamp.

Generally the wedges are more controllable than simply clamping a crack with Perspex. The wedges help to align the broken edges.

Stretcher clamps

Many repairers use stretcher clamps, which apply pressure across the face of the violin and help pull the crack together. They are bent to the profile you need. There is less control with a stretcher clamp, but they can be very useful additions to the crack repairer's arsenal.

BELOW Stretcher clamps.

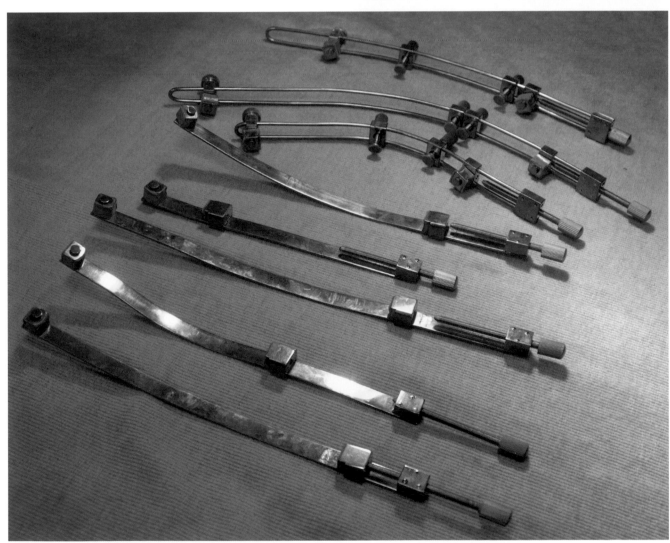

ABOVE Using a stretcher clamp.

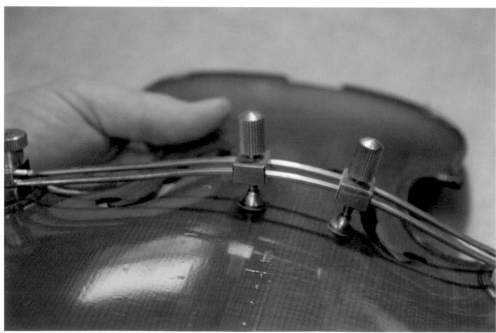

LEFT The feet on a stretcher clamp have cork on them to protect the violin surface.

End-crack clamps

End-crack clamps are useful for pulling together the end of a crack. Their design allows them to grip the edges and a mechanism then pulls the two grips together.

Missing wood

It is rarely necessary to add wood to a crack and the problem with introducing new wood is that it is difficult to get a good match. Even if the wood has been eaten away by woodworm, even by as much as 1mm, it is still possible to bring the edges of the crack together by using progressively warmer water in the crack. The water swells the wood and allows you to pull the edges together.

Fitting studs

To strengthen the crack it is common practice to fit permanent studs, which are fixed across the crack and shaped and blended with the violin plate to be aesthetically pleasing. They are specially fitted and aligned for maximum strength and reinforcement.

Once the glued crack has dried, remove the temporary studs and temporary gluing blocks in preparation to add permanent studs.

For studs on the back plate, maple or willow can be used as alternatives to spruce, but only use spruce for the front. Begin by squaring up a good length of spruce, with its squared dimensions made to suit the size of the studs you want to fit.

ABOVE End-crack clamp.

Take a guess at how many studs you will need for the crack and cut your length of spruce accordingly, allowing for each stud to be 4–5mm thick. The studs will be shaped after fitting so the thickness is not critical, but do not make them too thin.

Mark a line running down the back of the piece, and an arrow on the top. This will help you to ensure that each cleat on the crack will face the same way.

BELOW Stud making.

BELOW Shaping a stud.

BELOW Chalk-fitting a stud.

Mark out 30mm spaces along the centre of the crack, and chalk-fit each stud in turn. With each block you will be chalk-fitting one side to the inner surface of the front, and on the top of the block you will need to number them sequentially. If you are doing several cracks at once, it is good to use alternate sequences, such as 1–2–3–4 and a–b–c–d. Sequential numbering is another aid to keeping yourself organised when you have a pile of fitted blocks, and makes your work more efficient.

Do not cut the studs too thinly because when you apply glue to a thin stud it will want to lift and curl, so make each one at least 4–5mm thick. Cut them with a sharp chisel right on to the bench, into the end grain of the stud. You will slice a nice stud with this method, but just ensure your fingers are not in range!

The line you drew on the spruce stick will give you the direction of the block you just cut off without having to peer at it too closely. Invariably the studs like to pop off the chisel and land on the floor, so it is good to have this indication mark when you locate it again.

Stylistically it is nice to have the sides at a slight angle because this looks aesthetically pleasing. The main thing to check is that the grain is across the crack because this will add the extra strength you need in the repair.

Once all studs are fitted and marked up, start warming up the glue and get ready to glue them on. Clean off any residue chalk before fitting.

When the studs are being glued on, be careful not to get glue on your fingers. The problem occurs when you are pressing down on a stud for a minute, with a glue-laden finger, while the glue dries. When you remove your finger, more often than not the stud will stay on it and not on the crack. As an alternative, you can use a strip of Perspex or cork on the outside of the instrument, and use clamps to hold the studs on while the glue dries. Somehow this seems overly cumbersome for gluing a tiny piece of wood.

Leave the studs for four hours, or even better overnight, for the glue to thoroughly set, and then you are ready to shape the studs.

The best practice is to shape a stud as a dome so that it is higher in the middle, and use a wine cork and some 400-grit wet-and-dry paper to remove the facets from shaping. Each side has a feathered edge, so it blends nicely with the plate. Try not to abrade the front while you are shaping the studs. A nice crisp bevel on the end grain sides completes the work.

ABOVE Making studs.   **BELOW** Aligning studs.

Regluing plates

When a plate has come unstuck, this is characterised by a buzzing sound emanating from the body of the violin. If you tap around the plate with your knuckle, you should be able to detect from the 'bzzzz' sound precisely where it has come unstuck. Plates come unstuck when the glue fails, and, of course, when they have been removed to facilitate a repair.

ABOVE A slightly open plate.   **BELOW** A truly open plate.

Regluing plates

For this task you will need:

- A thin artist's palette knife.
- Closing clamps.
- Glue.
- Kitchen towel.

1 Set up your repair process in a warm, draught-free room, the warmth being useful to give you more working time with the glue. As always, make sure your work area is clean, so you do not end up gluing dust and other bits to your violin.

2 Position closing clamps – specialist clamps used to apply even pressure around the edge of a violin when gluing plates – on the violin where needed, and loosely tighten them to make sure they are placed well in order to close the gap properly.

3 You can use a block with some cork and a couple of clamps to secure the plate on the bottom block.

4 Heat up some glue, remembering to keep it nice and thin and hot. Using thin glue means that future repairs will be simpler, because it will be easier to separate the plate. If you use strong glue, someone in the future may have trouble getting the plate off, and in the process may damage the violin.

5 When the glue is ready, take your palette knife and dip it in, allowing excess glue to drip off, and then slide the palette knife into the gap. The thinness of a palette knife makes it particularly suitable for getting glue into a tight space.

6 Try to work cleanly and always wipe away excess glue with kitchen towel while it is still fluid. If glue dries on varnish, it will take off the varnish if it is picked at.

7 Once you are happy with your glue application, tighten the clamps to finger tightness, and clean off any more glue that seeps out. Keep the clamps on for at least eight hours, preferably overnight, so that the glue takes hold properly.

8 Finally undo the clamps and check over the joint visually and also by tapping near the problem to make sure it has been solved.

Spiral peg bushing

Spiral peg bushing is an alternative method of repair to a worn peg hole. It is a better method of peg bushing than the one described in the previous chapter ('Intermediate maintenance') because less wood is removed from the original peg box and it is much stronger.

1 A shaving of maple about 2–3mm thick is taken along the grain ready for gluing.

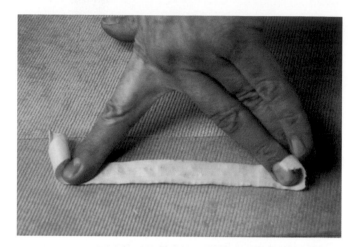

2 The shaving is prepared for gluing on a piece of flat Perspex and the entire shaving is covered with glue, using a good brush.

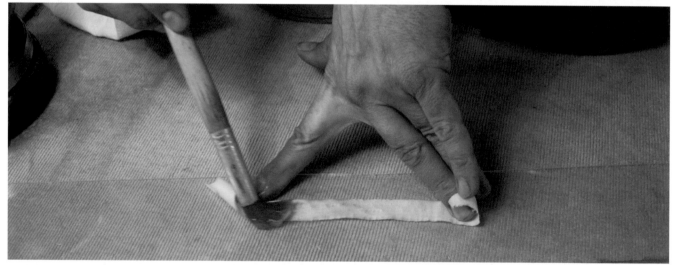

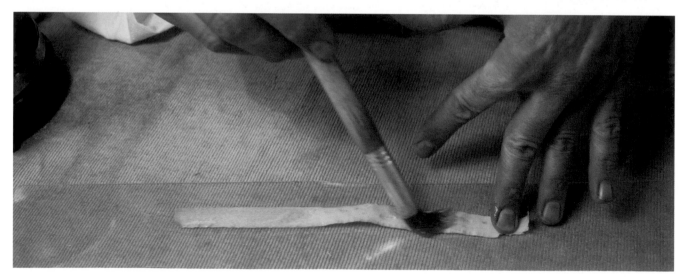

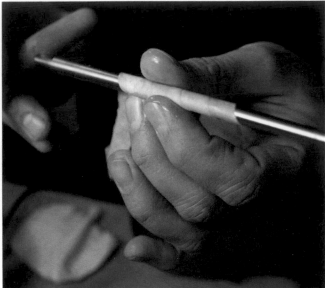

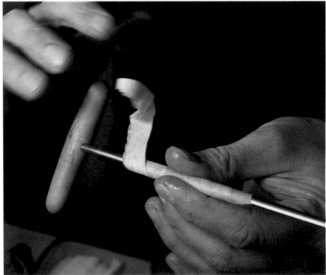

3 The shaving is then wound around a taper with the glue side outwards. This must be done reasonably quickly because the glue will begin to dry as soon as it is off the heat, and you need good adhesion in the peg box.

4 The taper is then put into the peg hole and wound back to allow the spiral of wood to adhere to the inside of the peg hole.

5 The taper is then withdrawn, leaving the shaving behind. The shaving is allowed to dry in the peg hole, after which it can easily be trimmed back.

6 This process can be repeated for as many layers of wood that you need to effect the repair, but a nice long shaving will give you good thickness in any case.

Appendices

Standard measurements (full-size violin)

Body length	355mm
Upper bout width	167mm
Middle bout width	112mm
Lower bout width	208mm
Rib height	30–32mm
Thickness of plates at the edges	3–4mm
Purfling edge offset	4mm
Plate top to nut	130mm
Body stop	195mm
Lining thickness	2.1mm
Lining height	8mm
Bass bar thickness	5.5mm
Fingerboard length	270mm
Fingerboard thickness at edge	5.5mm
Fingerboard nut width	24mm
Fingerboard bottom width	43mm
Peg box nut width	24–24.5mm
Peg box top width	20mm
Sound post diameter	6mm

Note These are the basic standard (average) measurements. Arching heights are omitted because these are particular to the maker, and so there is not really an average.

Tool plans

In this section we include tools you can make at home from simple materials that will greatly aid you in your repair and set-up work.

Bridge Templates

Bridge and string height guide templates can be made out of thin ply, or any suitable scrap wood you have.

Lines marked E and G

To use the bridge template, clip it onto the front of the bridge and sight down the fingerboard, the edge of the finger board should line up with the lines on the template. The space between those lines and top of bridge then give the desired string heights.

Left hand nick

The nick on the lefthand side can be placed onto the top of the bridge and will give the thickness of the bridge all the way along.

The angled side goes towards the front of the bridge.

Larger nick cutout

The larger cut out gives the width of the bridge foot.

Extra useful information

- Violin Inter-String Distance = 11.2mm at the bridge, and 5.1mm at the Nut.
- Viola Inter-String Distance= 13.mm at the bridge , and 5.8mm at the Nut.
- Cello Inter-String Distance = 15mm at the bridge, and 7.8mm at the Nut.

Staggered Template

The staggered guide is a useful check for string heights at the end of the fingerboard near the bridge.

The thinner steps are the lower strings on the violin viola cello, the larger steps are the higher strings.

Place the guide under the strings at the end of the finger board to check.

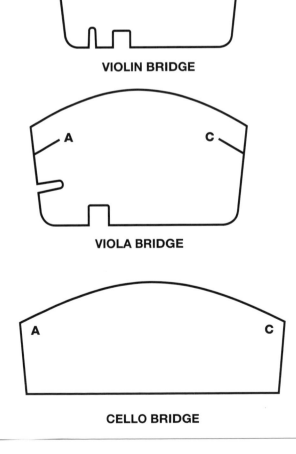

VIOLIN BRIDGE

VIOLA BRIDGE

CELLO BRIDGE

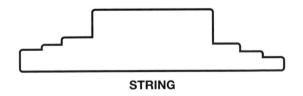

STRING

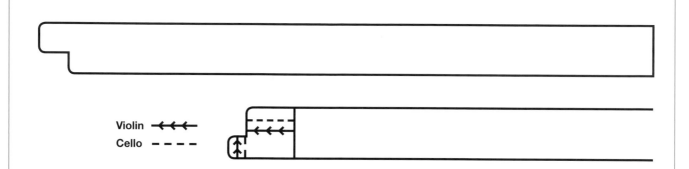

Violin ←←←
Cello – – – –

Sound post tool

The sound post tool can be made out of brass or any suitable thin flexible sheet metal, we used 0.3mm brass. It is used to guage the position of the sound post relative to the bridge feet.

To construct the tool rivet the two pieces together so that the smaller piece is aligned with the larger piece as shown in the section on template tools.

The chevronned lines relate to the violin and viola, the dashed lines relate to the cello.

The longer strip of the tool is placed into the f-hole on the treble side so that nick in the strip caresses the sound post.

The upper strip of the tool then gives you the position of the bridge with respect to the sound post.

The long arrows relate to the back of the bridge, and the short arrows show the position of the side of the bridge with respect to the sound post.

Fingerboard curvature

These tools can be used to check the curvature of the fingerboard, they are simply placed on top of the fingerboard and allow you to see any irregularity in fingerboard shape.

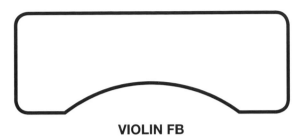

VIOLIN FB

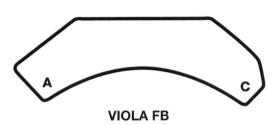

VIOLA FB

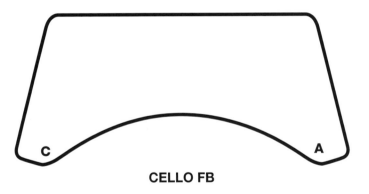

CELLO FB

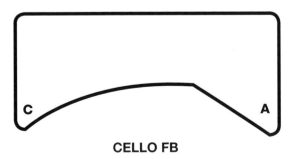

CELLO FB

Further reading and resources

Books ('affordable' price range)

The Art of Violin Making, Chris Johnson and Roy Courtnall (Robert Hale, 1999)
Perhaps the best book on modern violin making at the time of writing.

Violin Making: A Practical Guide, Juliet Barker (Crowood, 2001)
A book with some very nice violin-making photography.

The Violin Makers: Portrait of a Living Craft, Mary Anne Alburger (Victor Gollancz, 1978)
A really good read about modern violin makers and their craft.

Stradivarius: Five Violins, One Cello and Three Centuries of Enduring Perfection, Toby Faber (Random House, 2006)
A wonderful exploration of some of Stradivari's instruments, eminently readable and recommended casual reading.

The Red Book, Donald M. Cohen
A comprehensive history of auction prices for violins, updated once a year.

The Physics of the Violin, Lothar Cremer (MIT Press, 1985)
Heavy for some, but a thorough technical examination of how the violin works acoustically.

Violin-Making: As It Was, And Is, Edward Heron-Allen (Cassell, 1958)
A good historical read about violin making, eccentric and quirky at times.

Traité de Lutherie, François Denis (www.traitedelutherie.com)
If you are interested in how the violin outline is designed, this is the book for you.

Tools for Woodwork: The Sharpening, Care and Use of Hand Tools, Charles H. Haywood (1946)
Some good general information on woodworking tools and how to use them.

Books ('connoisseur' price range)

Antonio Stradivari four-volume compendium with DVD (http://www.stradivaribooks.com).
The best photographic work recording the craftsmanship of Stradivari; very expensive, but unsurpassed.

The Secrets of Stradivari, Simone F. Sacconi (Libreria del Convegno, 1979)
A detailed investigation of the work of Stradivari, and how things were done – or probably done – by the master maker.

Violin Restoration: A Manual for Violin Makers, Hans Weisshaar and Margaret Shipman (Weisshaar and Shipman, 1988)
An excellent book on repair and restoration techniques.

The Conservation, Restoration and Repair of Stringed Instruments and Their Bows, edited by Tom Wilder (Archetype Publications, 2011)
This 3 volume set is an excellent collection of articles on instrument restoration and repair.

Magazines and journals

There are two excellent violin-related monthly magazines: *The Strad* in the UK and *Strings* in the USA. *The Strad* often contains articles about old violins and also twice a year gives away violin-making pattern posters, which contain all the critical measurements from interesting instruments. With such a poster, a violin maker is able to make a good copy of the original violin. It is also worth checking out the online Strad bookshop (http://www.orpheusmusicshop.com/books), where you will find some very detailed books on a variety of violin-related subjects, including the following:

The Strad Library: The Best of Trade Secrets (two volumes)
Good articles on construction techniques.

Strad Special Editions
Good articles on some famous instruments.

Online resources

There are also some very good online resources. One we highly recommend is the Library of Congress for its excellent photography of instruments. Here you will find some superb high-resolution photographs of Stradivari, Amati and Guarneri violins.
http://lcweb2.loc.gov/diglib/ihas/html/instruments/strings-home.html

Glossary

This section explains terminology that you may come across when talking with makers, restorers and dealers.

Arching The carving out of the outside profile of the violin for the front and back.

Arching template Used when arching the violin, a set of templates that define the profile of the violin along its length and in cross section at various key points.

Bee-sting The tip of the purfling at each of the four corners on the C-bout.

Bending iron A specially shaped hot iron for bending ribs or linings into the gentle curves of the violin.

Brazil wood Wood commonly used for making bows; not quite as good as Pernambuco.

Bushing Bushing is a method of filling out worn holes with new wood, so that they can be redrilled. There are several methods of bushing.

Eye The small central part of the violin scroll volute.

Graft A costly repair whereby a neck or scroll is grafted on to the violin to replace a broken one.

Grain This is related to the direction of growth of the tree: straight-grained wood, where the tree has grown straight and evenly, is the best for violin fronts.

Ground A pigment or dye that is first put on to a violin before

the coats of varnish are applied. This soaks into and colours the wood to provide a basis for the colour of the violin. Because varnish is translucent, a good violin finish will allow colours from different layers to come through the coats of varnish, providing a wonderful quality of depth to the finish.

Hollowing The process by which the inside of the violin is carved out.

Luthier Originally a term used to describe a lute maker, but now widely used to describe a maker of any stringed instruments.

Madder A brown-to-red dye derived from processing the root of the madder plant, commonly used in making varnish pigments.

Medullary rays These are arranged perpendicular to a tree's growth rings, and when a tree is alive they are used to transport nutrients. As indicators of strength, medullary rays are important in bridge and neck construction, among other things.

Pernambuco The best wood for making bows, having the required spring, weight and density beloved by bow makers.

Resin Used by violin makers in making varnish.

Rosin Used on the bow to facilitate the playing of the violin.

Thicknessing The process of reducing the violin front and back to its final thickness to allow the wood to resonate properly.

Volute The three-dimensional spiral shape of the scroll.

Wolf note An unintended sound that emanates from the instrument in sympathy with another note.

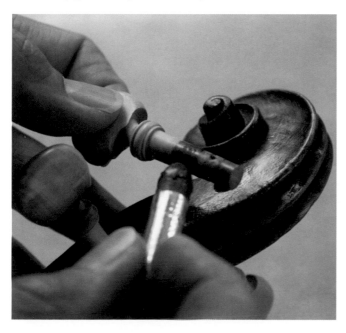

Index

Page numbers given in *italics* indicate the presence of a photograph or illustration.

Author acknowledgements

The authors would like to acknowledge the following who have been involved either directly or indirectly in putting together this book:

With special thanks to:
The Chi Mei Museum, Taiwan and Wong Man Fai Andy, Hong Kong
Bevan Wulfenstein and Alma Jay Young of Wulffenstejn Hardanger Fiddle & Mandolin Works, Utah, USA
Paul and Liz Gosling

Marcus would also like to thank Paul Bowers of Bowers Violins, Edinburgh for his encouragement and support, and everyone at the Newark School of Violin Making.
John would also like to thank Laurens Huige for all his hard work at the Chapel.